The Gopher Tor
A Life History

Patricia Sawyer Ashton and Ray E. Ashton Jr.

Pineapple Press, Inc.
Sarasota, Florida

We dedicate this book to Joan Berish, whose personal dedication to the conservation of this species for so many years has had many significant impacts at all levels within research, protection, and education. Most of all, we thank her for her constant encouragement.

We further dedicate this book to our nieces, nephews, and our grandson, who all love tortoises. They represent the future generations who may not have the opportunity to enjoy the gopher tortoise as adults unless greater efforts are made in gopher tortoise conservation and habitat management.

Inquiries should be addressed to:

Pineapple Press, Inc.
P.O. Box 3889
Sarasota, Florida 34230

www.pineapplepress.com

Library of Congress Cataloging-in-Publication Data

Ashton, Patricia Sawyer.
   The gopher tortoise : a life history / by Patricia Sawyer Ashton and Ray E. Ashton, Jr.—1st ed.
         p. cm. – (Life history series)
   Includes bibliographical references.
   ISBN 1-56164-303-3 (hardback : alk. paper) – ISBN 1-56164-301-7 (pbk. : alk. paper)
1. Gopher tortoise. I. Ashton, Ray E. II. Title. III. Series.

QL666.C584A85 2004
597.92'4—dc22

                                                            2004046503

First Edition
10 9 8 7 6 5 4 3 2 1

Design by Patricia S. Ashton and Shé Heaton
Printed in China

The Gopher Tortoise
A Life History

Acknowledgments

Over the years many people have worked with us or encouraged us in our efforts to do research on gopher tortoises and to develop conservation and education efforts to help gopher tortoises. Beginning in the 1970s we were encouraged to work on tortoise burrows and foraging behavior by Walter Auffenberg and Dick Franz. We hand-excavated our first burrows, collected data on the commensals in the burrows, and analyzed tortoise feces, providing data to Dr. Auffenberg. This difficult work was done with the help of many junior curators at the Florida State Museum. Some years later we began working with a number of people gathering data and supporting the efforts of the developing Gopher Tortoise Council and later founded Finca de la Tortuga–Ashton Biological Preserve, the Ashton Biodiversity Research and Preservation Institute and its major project, and the Gopher Tortoise Conservation Initiative.

Along with the two people named above, we would like to acknowledge the encouragement and help of professionals, friends, and colleagues including Bob Mount, Lynn Mosura-Bliss, Dale Jackson, Ken Dodd, Peter Pritchard, the late Duke Campbell, Steve Christman, Bruce Means, Jim Stevenson, Bob Mount and especially Joan Berish (then Diemer). Also we extend our profound thanks to those biologists who peer-reviewed this book.

Also in the early years when tortoise conservation was just beginning to take shape, a number of people in the Florida Game and Fresh Water Fish Commission (now the Florida Fish and Wildlife Conservation Commission), especially Rick McCann, Don Wood, and Brad Hartman, were extremely helpful. Others that have been instrumental in keeping us going with our research at the preserve include Elliott Jacobson, Paul Klein, Dave Rostal, Henry Mushinsky, Earl McCoy, Craig Guyer, Kristin Berry, and Jeff Lovich. Grace McLaughlin, Mary Brown, J.R. Hand, and Becky Smith have contributed much to our understanding and efforts. We also need to thank so many students, interns, and neighbors, especially Russ Elliott, who have helped over the years to collect data on tortoises, their burrows, and forage. We thank past students who from their current professions have provided us with important questions that have helped give our tortoise research direction. In particular we appreciate the help of Inik and Brad Smith, Barbara Burgeson, Kim Trebasky, and Maurine Booness, who have provided us with the questions that have led to researching answers on tortoise management. We especially want to thank those who have helped us collect data or who have provided data over the years as well as those who have provided encouragement for us to continue our work. These include David Lee, Lora Smith, George Heinrich, Richard Owens, Ghislaine Guyot, Lyn Phou, and Milena Scholtens Moreira. We particularly want to thank Holly Mayo, Sharon Karsen, Mr. and Mrs, Jim Bierly, and the other Gopher Tortoise Conservation Initiative volunteers and landowners who have joined the Gopher Tortoise Reserve Program for all their assistance and prodding to keep this program alive.

We also wish to acknowledge the thousands of people that we have talked over the phone, on the Internet, and at workshops and programs regarding their concerns and questions about tortoises and conservation. From these we have identified the most frequently asked questions and tried to make sure to include answers. There are so many who have been supportive and helped in many ways that we are unable to list everyone and beg forgiveness if someone feels forgotten.

Finally we wish to thank Mr. M.C. Davis, Santa Rosa Beach, Florida, whose financial and personal support nudged us into creating the Gopher Tortoise Conservation Initiative, a program of the Ashton Biodiversity Research and Preservation Institute, Inc. We also thank the Gopher Tortoise Council for its financial support and work done toward the same goals.

Preface

The gopher tortoise is an excellent representative of all the upland wildlife in the Southeast and in fact throughout the world. As human needs for space increase, we divide the habitat with roads and then fill in the space between with homes, shopping centers, and schools. Once where there were many square miles of open wild lands required by so many species—today these are shrinking into small parcels of land barely large enough to support the gopher tortoise and many of its associated species.

Because of this rapid development it is more important than ever that people of all ages realize that if we wish to have some of these species around for the next generations, we must learn about their needs and begin to plan for the open space they and their habitats require throughout the southeastern United States. Many people, including families and young people, have been shocked to learn that such a passive animal as the gopher tortoise can be destroyed at such an alarming rate. They wish to become part of the solution, not just part of the problem. We hope that this book will help these people become involved.

The first step in becoming a positive force in conservation is to become educated. Until now, there have been no books where people could learn about the gopher tortoise, how it lives, and its habitat requirements. We have researched many scientific papers and have presented the findings of these papers. We have many years of research and observations, and we provide that here so that much of what we know is available to the general public. It is our hope that this publication is written in a simple way that can be understood by both adults and young students who wish to learn about this fascinating species. We hope this will encourage them to begin to work in their states, counties, and communities to make sure that there continue to be places for generations of tortoises in order that future human generations may appreciate and learn from them.

Patricia and Ray Ashton

Meet the Gopher Tortoise

What is it? Can I touch it?

Look...It's a gopher tortoise!

Gopher tortoises can most easily be seen when they cross the road, feed at the roadside, sit in the sun at a burrow mouth, or come into a yard to forage. Tortoises may stop and pull their head and legs into their shell when approached. They can run pretty fast for short distances when frightened and may dive into their burrow to get away or they may move into the shadows of grasses or larger plants keeping very still so they seem to disappear.

Can I touch it?
Will it hurt me?
Will touching it hurt it?

Gopher tortoises are not harmful to humans. They usually don't try to bite even when picked up. They do have very strong, muscular legs with claws that can scrape and scratch. Sometimes when picked up tortoises will eliminate, making a smelly mess in order to frighten off predators. You can look at a tortoise, but you really should leave it alone. If it is in the middle of the road and likely to be run over, **an adult** can move it off to the side of the road it was headed for so it won't try to cross again.

Elizabeth and her son Xander observe a gopher tortoise crossing the road. Xander was amazed to see it "freeze" as a car approached.

State and federal governments have rules designed to protect gopher tortoises and other species from being injured or destroyed by human activities. These rules make it illegal to take a gopher tortoise home or dig up its burrow or disturb its daily life. Scientists, educators, land managers or consultants may get a **permit** to allow them to work more directly with the gopher tortoise. It is okay for you to observe a tortoise, but don't interfere with its activities or take one home.

How can I learn more about you and what you do?

Think about the questions you would like to have answered about gopher tortoises and how they live their lives. Here are some questions you might ask:

1. What are you?
2. Who were your ancestors?
3. How did you survive until now?
4. Who are your enemies?
5. Is your shell your home?
6. In what habitats can I find you?
7. Where are your burrows?
8. How can I know if you are at home?

9. Who else lives in your burrow?
10. Why are burrows important?
11. What do you eat?
12. How do you communicate?
13. Where do you go in a forest fire?
14. Where do you lay eggs?
15. How do you find a mate?

Scientists have been studying gopher tortoises for many years. We have learned many things about how they eat, mate, lay eggs, and dig burrows. There are still many things we do not know. We do not completely understand how they communicate, why they choose to change burrows, or how they select food. We have included information gathered by many scientists as well as from our research.

Ray Ashton studies an adult gopher tortoise that lives on Ashton Biological Preserve outside Archer, Florida.

Nearly 1-year-old hatchling

Tortoises come in many shapes and sizes. An **adult** can be bigger than a dinner plate while a **hatchling** comes out of an egg a little larger than a golf ball.

Adult tortoises can be yellowish-brown, dark brown, or deep gray. **Juveniles**—those in between hatchlings and adults—can be yellowish, tan, or light gray. The pattern (shapes and color on the scales) on hatchlings is distinctive. How would you describe this pattern?

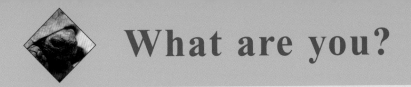

What are you?

Tortoises are turtles adapted for living on land.

Scientific (taxonomic) Classification

Phylum: Chordata (has a spinal cord)

Vertebrate (has bony vertebrae)

Class: Reptilia (has scales, produces amniotic eggs, and is ectothermic)

Order: Testudines (has flattened and fused bones—ribs and vertebrae—to form a shell covered by dermal scutes. Anapsid (does not have skull openings for jaw muscles)

Family: Testudinoidea (has clawed, elephantine hind feet and no webs between toes)

Genus: *Gopherus* means "burrower"

Species: *polyphemus* means "lives in cave" (Greek) or "many-voiced" (Latin)

The scientific name of the gopher tortoise is Gopherus polyphemus

(pronounced "go-FUR-us pol-ee-FEE-mus")

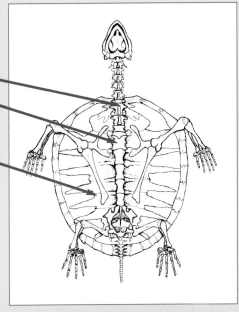

Tortoises and turtles have large scales on their shells called scutes.

Gopher tortoises are classified or grouped together with all the turtles in the order Testudines. Turtlelike fossils have been found from the early Triassic (250 million years ago), but the gopher tortoise is the only land turtle or tortoise species (of family Testudinoidae) remaining in the southeastern United States after these hundreds of thousands of years.

Scutes

Gular scute

Scales

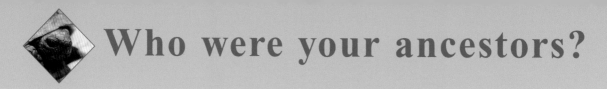

What were the early tortoise species in the southeastern U.S. like?

Turtles that looked very much like those we see today (with dermal plates or scutes covering a bony carapace) were alive in the Triassic, when dinosaurs roamed the earth. By the Jurassic, turtles existed that could pull their head, tail, and feet into their shell, and instead of teeth they had a bony beak. The Tertiary Period in southeastern North America saw diverse turtle and tortoise species with both giant tortoises (like *Hesperotestudo incise*) and very small ones (like *Floridemys nana*). The information gathered by paleontologists when they unearthed the fossils of the giant *Hesperotestudo* tortoises indicates that they probably did not use burrows. The habitats of southeastern North America were at times much wetter with lots of lush vegetation. We can guess that these giant tortoises may have behaved much like present-day Galapagos or Aldabra tortoises (shown below). They depended upon their size for protection as adults, and as juveniles they were good at hiding.

Aldabra tortoise

Relative size of giant tortoise to gopher tortoise

Predecessors of today's gopher tortoise appeared in the Tertiary Period. The gopher tortoise appeared in the Quaternary Period during the middle to late Pleistocene Epoch.

Periods and epochs	Years ago	Predecessor
Permian Period	245 to 286 million	Early reptiles
Triassic Period	250 to 208 million	
Jurassic Period	208 to 144 million	Turtlelike reptiles
Cretaceous Period	66 to 144 million	Modern sea turtles
Tertiary Period	66 to 2 million	Many species of turtles and tortoises
Paleocene Epoch	58 to 66 million	
Eocene Epoch	37 to 58 million	Giant and small turtle species
Oligocene Epoch	24 to 37 million	
Miocene Epoch	5 to 24 million	
Pliocene Epoch	2 to 5 million	
Quaternary Period	2 million to present	
Pleistocene Epoch	500,000 to 2 million	Gopher tortoise
Holocene Epoch	recent to 500,000	

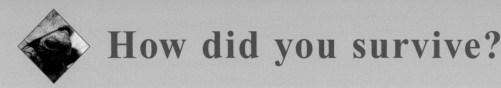

How did you survive?

What happened to the other tortoise species in the southeastern U. S.? When did the gopher tortoise appear and why did only the gopher tortoise survive?

We are not sure about the answer to the first question, but we do know that early humans lived in the same places that the ancient tortoises lived and were there at the time the other species of tortoises became extinct. Humans probably **hunted** them for food. Could humans have killed too many tortoises so that the species became extinct? Research shows that humans are still endangering tortoises today by eating them and **taking away their habitat**. We also know there were many **climatic changes** at the time these species disappeared. Changes in climate can alter plant growth and tortoises are primarily herbivores, so they are dependent upon the presence of sufficient, healthy vegetation. Long-term and widespread changes in climate may have caused many of the animals and plants that lived at that time to go extinct, including some species of tortoise.

Fossil Tortoises of Southeastern U.S.

Species	Originated during	Size
Hesperotestudo incise	late Pleistocene	small
Hesperotestudo mlynarski	early–mid Pleistocene	small
Hesperotestudo crassiscutata	Pleistocene	giant
Hesperotestudo hayi	early Pliocene	giant
Hesperotestudo alleni	late Miocene	small
Floridemys nana	Miocene	tiny

We do have a good idea of the probable answer to the second question—Why did the gopher tortoise survive when the other species died out?

Gopher tortoises dig **burrows** and this made them different from the other species that died out. Scientists think that the other tortoises did not dig deep burrows into the ground. Many tortoises today make shallow cavities, sometimes called "palates," in dirt and under vegetation. But these would not provide the same level of protection as the deep burrows that Gopher tortoises still dig today.

The gopher tortoise, *Gopherus polyphemus*, appeared in the middle to late Pleistocene. This species was distinct from several older unnamed taxa (groups of genetically distinct animals) found in Florida.

Is your shell your home?

The gopher tortoise's shell is part of its body, not its home.

Gopher tortoises pull their head into their shell and then pull in their armored legs to cover their head and the opening. They cannot take off their shell and walk away as in a cartoon.

Their shell is made of bone. Their backbone and ribs are flattened and fused to the bony shell which is covered with **scutes**.

The **burrow** is the tortoise's home. The **shell** is part of the tortoise and it is not removable without killing the animal.

The shell acts as **armor**, providing physical protection, particularly for adult tortoises. Its color and shape help the tortoise to blend into the soil, grass clumps, and general background. This **camouflage** provides additional protection from possible predators. The shell is also used in regulation of body temperature. In adults it is generally dark in color and absorbs heat, which is then distributed around the body. Tortoises, like most reptiles, are **ectothermic** (cold-blooded). Basking in the sun is necessary to raise the body temperature to an optimal level for the healthy function of the tortoise's body systems. The heavy shell of the tortoise requires very strong leg muscles for movement and to turn itself back over if it is flipped on its back.

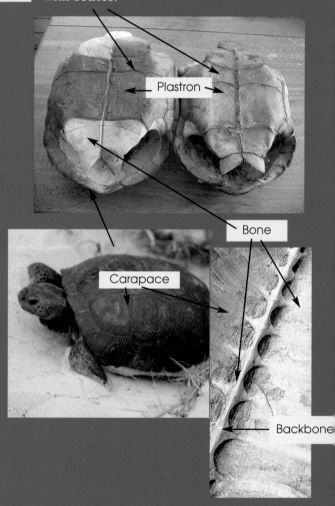

Plastron

Bone

Carapace

Backbone

Tail

Anal scutes

Plastron

Gular scutes

Bridge

The tortoise's shell is covered with scutes made of a special hardened substance called keratin (similar to your finger nails) which is formed in the epidermis. These scutes grow outward from the center forming rings, but these rings are not a dependable way to tell the age of the tortoise.

II. The Burrow

Why is the burrow the tortoise's home?
Where are burrows found?

Tortoises depend upon burrows for shelter, and they serve as a **home**. Tortoises depend on surrounding habitats to provide food and water. Just like some people may have a home in town and a vacation home or may use a motel for vacation, tortoises may use more than one burrow over time. Scientists discovered this by recapturing or radio tracking or observing tortoises using burrows in more than one place. Finding the burrows used by one specific tortoise is a lot of work!

The burrows used by a tortoise, its breeding territory, and its feeding area constitute the tortoise's **home range.** Tortoise burrows with nearby or overlapping home ranges in a given area are called a **cluster** and the tortoises that live there make up a **pod.** All the burrows being used at different times by the same tortoise may be in the same general area, particularly if there are land features (rivers, ravines) or human-made features like fences, buildings or roadways that restrict movement out of the area. When unrestricted, the tortoise may move a long distance to use a burrow for a while and then return.

Do tortoises live together in a burrow?

Adult tortoises do not usually share their burrows with other adults except in places where the conditions limit the number of burrows, as on islands. During the mating season male tortoises visit females in their burrows. Baby tortoises upon hatching may go into the adult burrow. Occasionally a juvenile may be found in an adult burrow.

All animals need
- **shelter**
- **food**
- **water**
- **space**

Being in a burrow under the sand is like being in an **underground shelter**. It provides a resting place safe from predators, and insulation from the heat or cold at the surface. Deeper burrows usually maintain a temperature above 13 degrees Celsius (55 Fahrenheit) in winter and below 28 degrees Celsius (80 Fahrenheit) in summer.

In which habitats should I look for gopher tortoise burrows?

Gopher tortoises live in **dry, sandy, upland and coastal areas of the southeastern United States** including Florida, Georgia, Alabama, Mississippi, southeastern Louisiana, and South Carolina.

Unlike aquatic turtles that live in or near water most of the time, tortoises live on **dry land.** Longleaf pine and turkey oak sandhills, pine flatwoods, pine savannah, coastal dune, barrier island, and oak scrub are the names of some of the natural **habitats** where tortoises can be found. They are also found in the red clay hills of the north Florida panhandle, and in southern Alabama and Mississippi. Yards, roadsides, and pastures are human-altered habitats where tortoises also may make burrows. Tortoises make their burrows in or near the places they will find **forage** (food). These habitats are usually open, sunny, and mostly in sandy soils. Burrows can be on roadsides, in open pastures, or at the edge of sandy beaches. They can also be hidden among palmettos, tree roots, shrubs, or in vine-covered, weeded areas.

There is a burrow in here!

Vine-covered shrubs and weeds

Sandhills and roadsides

Beaches, coastal dunes, and barrier islands

Can you find the tortoise burrow?

Tortoises prefer areas where there are lots of grasses and weeds with only 20–40% of the area covered by trees or shrubs.

What are the parts of a burrow?

Tortoise burrows usually consist of an apron, a mouth, a tunnel, and an end chamber. The **apron** is the dirt that has been piled in front of the burrow mouth. Most tortoise burrows have aprons, but some aprons are very small when the burrow is in soils with lots of shell or rock, such as on coastal beaches or in limerock areas. In flatwoods with a lot of palmettos the apron may be limited. Burrows in the clay hills of Georgia, western Alabama, and Mississippi may be hard to see with aprons not nearly as large as those found in the sandhills. The half moon–shaped **mouth** tells us the size of the tortoise that made the burrow (not necessarily the one who is living there now), and whether or not a tortoise is moving in and out of the burrow very often. Tortoise burrows almost never have more than one mouth; there is no escape hatch or back door. Read on to learn about the **tunnel** (page 13) and **end chamber** (page 15).

Why dig there?

We have no idea why a tortoise decides to start a burrow in a specific location.

There are two things we do know for certain:

1. They normally place the burrow mouth where the burrow gets some **sun** part of each day.
2. They like to put their burrows in soils that **drain well** and where the water table is low enough (at least two feet [60 cm] below the surface) to allow the burrow to **remain above water** during the wet season.

Tortoises also seem to prefer, when possible, to begin their burrows at the base of fences, logs, rocks, or palmettos, or where there are high areas, like roadsides and dirt spoil piles.

Burrow Mouth

Burrow Apron

We and others have studied whether or not the tortoise is using **compass direction**, slope of the land, or other cues for starting its burrow. We have found that they do not favor one particular compass direction. When we had students map the compass direction of the burrow mouth of all the burrows found by location, by soil type, by ground water table depth, by vegetative cover, and by habitat, we found burrows matching all points of the compass. In other words, there was no preferred direction and no correlation with other factors.

Imagine the work a tortoise does!

Tortoises dig their burrows by **using their front spadelike feet with strong claws**. First, a tortoise will dig with one foot, gouging out the soil several times and flipping it back behind. After several swipes, the tortoise changes sides and digs with the other leg. As the digging takes the burrow deeper underground, the tortoise will move backwards and use its front feet to sweep the soil farther up towards the mouth of the burrow. This developing **tunnel** will usually **slope** downwards at a ratio of 1 to 3, or for every 1 meter (3 feet) of depth the burrow extends 3 meters (9 feet) in length." As dirt piles up behind the tortoise in the tunnel, the tortoise will turn completely around and push the soil with the front of the shell and front feet, while using its strong pistonlike hind feet to push its body and the soil upwards to the mouth of the burrow. We have observed tortoises move soil out of the burrow in this manner and then turn around and appear to be wildly throwing the piles of soil out of the mouth of the burrow and onto the apron by flipping it with the front feet over their carapace and up into the air and out on to the apron.

If there are weeds in the way of final burrow mouth construction, we have observed tortoises maneuver the weed stem between the front leg, neck, and **gular** and then, pushing with great power from the hind legs, they will rock back and forth and even lift off the ground. Finally the weed roots will give way and the tortoise will carry the weed off of the apron before releasing it.

Notice the weed in the burrow mouth. This tortoise will actively work to keep its tunnel and burrow mouth clear.

...otice the soil freshly thrown out of a ...ewly dug burrow at the wooded ...dge of this longleaf pine –turkey oak ...ndhills habitat. Much of this huge ...il pile will be swept out over the ...rrounding land by the wind, rain, ...d movement of the tortoise in and ...t of the burrow over the next few ...eeks and months.

An adult tortoise's front feet are much smaller than this shovel used by humans to dig out a gopher burrow. It takes an adult tortoise an average of one day to dig 3 meters (9 feet) of burrow. This means in most areas, it takes about two or three days for a tortoise to complete a burrow down to the ground water table, which they almost always do. How long would it take you to dig a burrow 5 meters (15 feet) long and 2.6 meters (5 feet) deep?

How do biologists dig into and study gopher tortoise burrows?

Poles show direction of burrow.

4

1 **2**

3

Next it goes into a clean bin until all needed data can be taken.

Look how far below the ground some burrows can be! Poles are placed in the burrow to follow the direction of each segment so you know where to dig.

Success! After digging with a backhoe, by hand, and with shovels, the tortoise is out.

The first burrows biologists studied were **excavated** by hand which took a long time for the deep burrows in sandhills. The shallower burrows found in coastal areas and flatwoods were a little easier to dig. Samples of invertebrates were collected and the presence of vertebrates and signs of vertebrate use were noted as the burrow was carefully excavated.

Entomologists use strong vacuum cleaners with a very long hose to suck in the invertebrates from burrows. **Burrow scopes** with infrared cameras are used to look inside the dark burrow. This reveals interesting things like baby burrowing owls being eaten by snakes. Scopes also show burrow occupants like mice, opossums, snakes, and frogs.

It is not easy to use a burrow scope. Locating the burrow **end chamber** with a scope is difficult unless the operator is very experienced. The best way to follow a burrow completely to the end chamber and reveal its secrets and find the tortoise is to use a backhoe. This is a very delicate task that requires a highly trained operator on the backhoe and an expert directing the dig.

Display monitor and infrared camera

Burrow scopes (an infrared camera at the end of a long wire) can be used to see who may be occupying a narrow burrow. They are not useful for determining if the burrow is empty.

How deep is your burrow?

How does a gopher tortoise burrow look on the inside?

All tortoise burrows go **downward,** usually at a gentle 3 to 1 slope. They almost never go upward (except to get around a root or rock).

Eventually burrows end in an **end chamber** located at the opposite end of the burrow mouth. The end chamber is usually higher and wider than the tunnel. This is where the tortoise spends a great deal of time, although they will bask at the mouth and sit in the tunnel just down from the mouth.

The **depth** of a tortoise burrow depends on how far down the ground water table is located. This is usually around 3 meters (6 feet) below the ground surface but can be as far down as 7 meters (22 feet). Usually the deeper the water table, the deeper the burrow and the longer the tunnel.

The **length** of a burrow may be from 3 to 52 feet. The tortoise usually digs down to the ground water table so the burrow will maintain a high humidity and the end chamber will stay moist. In coastal areas and coarse, shell soils, the burrows may be shallow because the water table is close to the surface. Inland, the fine sandy soils of ancient dunes are very deep and the burrows may go down more than 20 feet.

We have found that tortoises are either right- or left-handed. A "right-handed" tortoise will dig a burrow that bends to the right as it slowly goes downward, while the burrow of a "left-handed" tortoise will bend to the left. Sometimes these turns are so sharp the burrow actually makes a spiral as it goes downward.

This burrow started at ground level (top right side of photo) and continued downward to more than 3 meters or 10 feet below the ground surface.

Burrow Mouth

End Chamber

The shape of the burrow (apron, mouth, and tunnel) helps the gopher tortoise hear sounds like footsteps and even rainfall—acting much like an old-fashioned "ear horn" by gathering sounds at the mouth and funneling them downward to the tortoise in the end chamber.

How do you know whether the hole you find is a gopher tortoise burrow or just a hole from a rotting tree stump or the burrow of another animal? What are the clues to look for?

There are clues that can help you identify a tortoise burrow from other holes in the ground. Active or recently active burrows are shaped like a half of a pie or a half moon. Why is this? Well, the **carapace** (top shell) of a gopher tortoise is rounded while the **plastron** (bottom) is nearly flat. The shape of the burrow is maintained when the tortoise rubs the top of the burrow with its carapace as it goes in and out of the burrow thus making the top of the burrow half round. The tortoise's bottom shell or plastron also continuously scrapes or flattens the bottom of the burrow.

Clue: A tortoise burrow has a flat bottom.

Clue: A tortoise burrow has a half-moon shaped top. This shapes is an **arch** which is a very strong shape used by human engineers when building bridges and buildings.

Of course, if you see a tortoise going in and out of a hole in the ground, it is probably a gopher tortoise burrow.

This tortoise is sideways in the burrow as it is in the process of turning around.

This scientist, called a herpetologist, is measuring the size of the gopher tortoise burrow with a special tool. The ends of the sticks are placed just inside the burrow; then the width of the burrow mouth can be read on the ruler below her hand so she doesn't have to bend over. The size of the burrow can tell us the size of the tortoise that made it or is currently maintaining it. The width of the burrow is slightly more than the length of the tortoise so the tortoise can turn around anywhere in the burrow.

Shape is one way to tell if a burrow is a gopher tortoise's or not.

A very rounded burrow is usually not a gopher tortoise's. Depending upon the size of the hole, **rounded burrows** usually are made by or are being used by armadillos, foxes, burrowing owls, or mice. Another way to determine if it is a tortoise burrow is by the **apron** of sand in front of the hole.

Are these gopher tortoise burrows?

Gopher tortoise burrow

Florida mouse burrow

Burrowing owl

Many animals take advantage of tortoise burrows and use them for their homes when the tortoise is gone. Armadillos may take burrows away from tortoises. They do this by redigging parts of the burrow and bringing in leaves for a nest. Sometimes a tortoise will actually get blocked in underground by the dirt moved by the armadillo. Gray foxes commonly use old tortoise burrows as dens to raise their young, as do coyotes and skunks. We found that Florida burrowing owls dig up old tortoise burrows to make their nest. These burrows stay cooler than the owl-dug burrows in the hot summer when the young are in the nest. Owls will occasionally move their fledging young from their nests to an occupied tortoise burrow to take advantage of the cooler temperatures and regularly cleaned burrow.

Gray fox

Mounds of sand (as shown below in a pasture) with small round openings or with no openings usually belong to the pocket gopher – a small mammal that makes extensive underground tunnels and in the process pushes up lots of sand piles. There are gopher tortoise burrows out in the field as well, but you have to examine them up close to tell the difference.

Armadillo

Geomys (pocket gopher) mounds

How do biologists find and classify burrows?

Burrows have been classified in the past as **active, inactive, and abandoned** by scientists and agencies that regulate what can be done around or to land where there are gopher tortoise burrows. The number of active and inactive burrows on a site has been used to calculate the expected number of tortoises on that land. But we now know that burrows previously classified as **abandoned** frequently provide shelter for hatchling and juvenile tortoises as well as for other protected species. We have added the term **"very inactive"** to these burrows and re-defined **abandoned** as having rooted vegetation in the mouth and no opening (or a collapsed opening) still visible.

Active

Clue: No obstructions in or around the opening.

Active

Clue: Distinct feeding trail leads to an active burrow.

Leaves in and over the mouth of this burrow and no tracks or fresh sand resulted in an **inactive** classification. But then we found that a juvenile was using this burrow.

Inactive

We now know that burrows previously classified as abandoned frequently provide shelter for hatchling and juvenile tortoises as well as other protected species. Snakes, spiders, insects, mice and lizards may also take up residence or simply use the burrow for temporary refuge from heat or cold or danger. Insects are more prevalent in burrows with some feces still in the end chamber.

Very Inactive

A **very inactive** burrow has almost no opening, and lots of leaves but no rooted vegetation in the mouth.

Clue: Lots of fresh sand pushed out onto apron. Tracks of tortoise, insects, lizards, or snakes in sand.

Active

Active

Clue: Noticeable tortoise foraging (feeding) area nearby.

Abandoned

Abandoned burrows may be collapsed and have rooted vegetation growing in the burrow mouth.

How do biologists find burrows?
How do they tell how many tortoises are in the area?

The biologist needs to have a good map and a good **aerial photograph** of the area being evaluated for tortoises. The aerial will reveal open savannah, coastal dunes, and grasslands where tortoises may make their burrows. In the field, the biologist will use a compass and **GPS** (Global Positioning System) unit to map the positions of burrows found during the survey by the team (1 scientist, 2 trained technicians). They actually walk straight lines called **transects** on the property, marking on maps and data sheets the details of what they find. They mark and classify all tortoise burrows (active, inactive, very inactive, or abandoned). The **projected number of tortoises** on the site is calculated using the currently accepted formula: number of active + inactive burrows times .67= projected # of tortoises. This is only an educated guess and until the tortoises are trapped or excavated the actual number is not really known. A much better estimate can be obtained by taking the total number of all tortoise burrows and dividing by two. Once we know the projected number of tortoises for a site we can make appropriate management and monitoring plans for the site or we can prepare a permit application for relocation or mitigation. Accuracy in counting burrows is very important for planning.

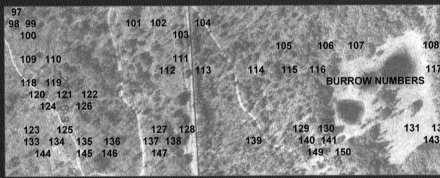

Aerial of site

BURROW NUMBERS

BURROW COUNT DATA	PROJECT Jones Tract

DATE July 10, 2003 WEATHER Cloudy, 94°F, No rain
TRANSECT NO. 12 A N→S TIME: START 10:15 FINISH 11:00A
SITE DESCRIPTION LLPine-Turkey Oak Savannah
TRANSECT DESIGNATION 12 A N→S
GPS (OR COMPASS HEADINGS): BEGINNING_____ END_____
CONDUCTED BY REA , PSA , KJA
PROJECT MANAGER REA   DATA VERIFICATION

BURROW NO.	QUAD OR TRANSECT	ACTIVE AGE CL	INACTIVE AGE CL	VERY INACTIVE	ABANDONED Ashton definition
134	12A03		Juv.		
135	12A07	Adult			
136	12A08		Adult		
137	12A12			✓	
138	12A21	Adult			
139	12A23	Adult			
140	12A26		Adult		
141	12A27			✓	
142	12A29			✓	
143	12A30	Juv.			
144	12A36		Adult		
145	12A40	Adult			
146	12A43	Adult			

* PERTINENT COMMENTS ON BACK

This data sheet (to the left) is used for recording the burrows found along a transect. The data would be entered into a computer and on a map. Global Positioning System (GPS) technology can be used to send coordinates directly into a computer map but it can only position burrows to within a meter or a few feet of their actual location. Note the burrows on the map to the right are clumped together in 5 **pods** or tortoise groups.

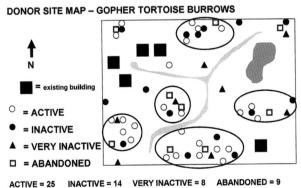

DONOR SITE MAP – GOPHER TORTOISE BURROWS

↑ N

■ = existing building

○ = ACTIVE
● = INACTIVE
▲ = VERY INACTIVE
□ = ABANDONED

ACTIVE = 25   INACTIVE = 14   VERY INACTIVE = 8   ABANDONED = 9

25 + 14 = 39 X .67 = 26 tortoises projected as being on site.

Prepared June 2003

What other animals may use a burrow when the tortoise is not using it?

Other animals, including frogs, toads, lizards, snakes, birds, rodents, other small mammals, spiders, and many invertebrates will use tortoise burrows on occasion to keep out of the cold or heat. They may also dash into a convenient burrow seeking cover when pursued by predators. We have found that quail or bobwhite use burrows frequently along with ground doves on cold nights. We have seen over-wintering warblers like redstarts, palm warblers, and prairie warblers catch flies that live in the burrow as they come out on sunny winter days. Toads and frogs prey on insects that come out at night.

Southern toad

Mole skink

Fence swift

Greenhouse frog

Wolf spider

Gopher frog

The higher humidity and favorable temperature range of the tortoise burrow can be very attractive to amphibians and invertebrates like insects and spiders.

The most common amphibians found in tortoise burrows are the greenhouse frog, the southern toad, and the gopher frog. Frogs, toads, lizards, and spiders are all predators on insects and invertebrates that may take shelter or reside in gopher tortoise burrows. Lizards are reptiles that occupy many niches in the same habitats where gopher tortoises are found. The fence swift and the mole skink can be found in or near burrows on occasion.

What snakes may use a burrow?

Most people have heard that various kinds of snakes can be found taking refuge, hunting for prey, or living in tortoise burrows. In the old days (late 1950s and before) you could commonly find diamondback rattlesnakes and indigo snakes in burrows. In the past, many tortoises were killed in rattlesnake round-ups when participants squirted gasoline into the burrows to force the rattlesnakes out.

Today, all species of snakes are not as common as they once were, perhaps because of too many roads crossing and cutting up the habitats and too much development replacing natural areas. The most common snakes we find today in tortoise burrows are the black racer and the eastern coachwhip. We still find diamondbacks and on a rare occasion a pigmy rattlesnake in burrows, but most of the snake species found associated with tortoise burrows are **nonvenomous** and harmless.

Diamondback rattlesnake

Pygmy rattlesnake

Southern hognose

Pygmy rattlesnakes and southern hognose snakes are often confused due to their spotted back pattern and small size. The hognose may flatten its head and hiss which adds to the confusion. Clue: The hognose has an up-turned pointed nose and no rattle

Black racer

Coachwhip

Crown snake

In the sand of the burrow apron and just inside the burrow mouth we find the tiny, tan-colored, black-headed crown snake, which eats centipedes.

Harmless snakes from burrows include the coachwhip, the southern hognose, the eastern hognose, and the red rat snake. The most common snake found in tortoise burrows is the southern black racer and the second most common is the coachwhip. All of these snakes feed primarily on small vertebrates like mice, frogs, toads, lizards, birds and other snakes. The hognose specializes in eating toads and the coachwhip chases lizards.

What vertebrates and invertebrates are adapted to using tortoise burrows?

Scientists study the creatures that inhabit or temporarily take refuge in gopher tortoise burrows. Herpetologist Dale Jackson published an article some years ago pointing out that more than 300 species use these burrows. Continued research has revealed a list of at least 400 species found in the burrows. This makes the tortoise very important in sustaining **biodiversity** in the treed grasslands (savannahs) throughout its range.

Research thus far has revealed that only a few of these 400 species are specifically adapted to using tortoise burrows. **Adapted species** are vertebrates and invertebrates that lived in prehistoric times alongside the tortoise and possibly other burrowing animals of the ancient savannahs of the Southeast. Some of these, like the gopher cricket and aphodius beetle, became **obligate species**, meaning they apparently only live in the tortoise burrow.

Other species are adapted to burrow life or to life with the gopher tortoise but can and do live elsewhere. They can be **parasites** like the gopher tick or **commensals** like the gopher frog, the federally protected indigo snake, Florida mouse, dung beetles, mites, spiders and small dung flies.

The Florida mouse makes small nest chambers off the side of the tortoise burrow tunnel and creates escape tunnels to the surface to avoid other visitors like the mouse-eating snakes (black racers, rat snakes, indigo snakes). The gopher frog will make burrows shaped like miniature gopher burrows along the side of the tortoise burrow or off the end chamber. These frogs eat big beetles and other insects and sit around the mouth of the gopher tortoise burrows.

Gopher cricket

Florida mouse

Gopher frog

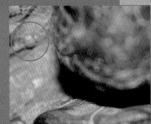
Gopher tick

Tortoise feces

The fact that the tortoise defecates in the end chamber is very important for many **obligate** species including gopher crickets, many different kinds of beetles, and small flies, all of which feed on tortoise feces (much like cave fauna that depend on bat guano). To date, many of these species have not been found anywhere else in the world while others have also been found in the Geomys (pocket gopher) tunnels.

We can find other animals when we dig tortoises out to study them or move them to a refuge. Their uplands habitat is being cleared so humans can use the land for houses or businesses. In the process of excavating the burrows herpetologists find many different organisms.

What is a keystone species?

How does the burrow make the tortoise a keystone species?

A tortoise burrow is very important to the habitat and the community because it provides shelter (and sometimes food) to 300–400 other species. So we call the gopher tortoise a **keystone species**.

Many kinds of invertebrates (worms, mollusks, crustaceans, insects, and spiders) and a variety of vertebrates (amphibians, reptiles, birds, and mammals) occupy the burrow made by a tortoise.

Also in these tortoise burrows scientists have found species that have been found nowhere else on planet Earth. Creatures like the gopher cricket or the tortoise burrow fly are obligate species, meaning they live only in tortoise burrows.

The term keystone comes from the most important stone in a structure without which the whole thing would fall down. A **keystone species** is one that is needed in a community or habitat for many other species to stay healthy and survive.

Burrows protect biodiversity

Some 300–400 species of mammals, birds, reptiles, amphibians, and invertebrates (various kinds of insects, spiders and other arthropods) have been found in tortoise burrows—of course, not necessarily all at the same time. Some of these animals (**obligates**) have been found only in burrows, while others are found elsewhere but may benefit by sharing the burrow (**commensals**), while others actually take over the tortoise burrow like the armadillo or the opossum. Some species only visit or take shelter occasionally, like some lizards and snakes. The **biodiversity** harbored by tortoise burrows is important to the **sustainability** (long-term survival) of the whole community in the habitats where burrows are found. Gopher tortoises and their burrows are currently protected by law. The enforcement of these laws protects not only the gopher tortoise but also the hundreds of creatures that depend on the tortoise's burrow.

Who may be in my burrow?

- gopher frog
- indigo snake
- burrowing owl
- black racer

- scorpions
- spiders
- mites
- ticks
- flies

- wolf spider
- gopher tick
- gopher cricket
- tortoise burrow fly

- Florida mouse
- diamondback rattlesnake
- coachwhip snake

- centipedes
- camel crickets
- gopher tortoise robber fly
- gopher tortoise copris beetle
- daddy longlegs
- millipedes
    - gopher tortoise aphodius beetle

How do you all get along?

How do snakes, mice, spiders, gopher frogs, owls, and others in the same burrow affect the gopher tortoise's daily life and each other?

The tortoise seems to be **undisturbed** by these co-inhabitants or occasional visitors, but we are still studying and trying to understand the effects these interactions have on the daily life and activities of the tortoise.

Most animals that go into a tortoise burrow are not there to eat. Most are seeking **shelter**. For this reason, they may not be in a feeding mode and may not take advantage of what is usually a prey species that is also in the burrow. Some predators follow potential prey into the burrow. How does this affect the tortoise? As a large herbivore, an adult tortoise has few predators. Most of the **potential predators** on adult tortoises are large mammals like dogs, coyotes and humans. Let's not forget cars and bulldozers!

Gopher cricket

Indigo snake

Red rat snake

Our research has shown that less than 4% of the over 5,000 tortoise burrows we collected data on have had snakes in them. Less than 20% have had small beetles but over 70% have had gopher crickets. In the proper habitats (scrub and sandhills) Florida mice were frequently found in burrows. In burrows within 1,000 meters of temporary ponds, gopher frogs were often found in burrows or out in the general area moving or feeding after dark.

Burrowing owl

Narrow-mouthed toad

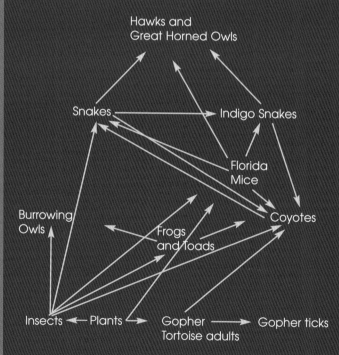

The gopher tortoise makes and maintains its burrow. Other organisms utilize the burrow in a variety of ways. How can they be in or around the burrow at the same time and not affect each other or the tortoise? They can't.

As part of the natural **community**, each of the species fills an important **niche** and plays a role. Some species, like the gopher tortoise, are **herbivores** and feed on plants. In turn, these plant eaters may be eaten by **carnivores** or be fed upon by **parasites**. And in turn, these carnivores will be eaten by other carnivores. All provide food for the **decomposers** when they die. Communities are made up of the interconnections of species called **food webs**. Baby gopher tortoises would probably be eaten by all of the carnivores in this food web but only the coyote or other large mammals will kill and eat an adult.

How We Learn About the Gopher Tortoise

How do we learn about you?

How can we capture the tortoise without harming the burrow?

What do we use can trapping for?

- To capture tortoises and other animals that go in and out of the burrow so we can obtain detailed data about their weight, size, health, parasites, blood, etc.
- To mark the tortoise and other burrow inhabitants so we can release and recapture them and learn about their daily movements.
- To move small numbers from a site (but this method is not recommended for relocation of large numbers of tortoises).

Tortoises are hard to catch outside of their burrow because they spend little time above ground, only 1-2 hours once every 2 or 3 days, depending on the habitat and the season.

Placing a correctly constructed and concealed bucket trap at the mouth of the burrow can help catch the tortoise as it goes into or comes out of it. This is called **bucket trapping** or **can trapping**.

A thin sheet of paper covered by sand hides the bucket so when the tortoise comes out or returns to the burrow it falls into the bucket trap.

The trap is shaded with branches or a board so when captured, the tortoise won't overheat in the sun.

Caught in a bucket trap!

Warning! Bucket trapping can be dangerous to tortoises if not done properly. The bucket must be large and deep enough to accommodate adults. It needs drainage holes so rainwater can't build up and drown a captured tortoise. Exposure to excessive heat or cold can kill a tortoise, so traps must be checked frequently (3 times daily) and properly shaded from direct sun. Only trained, skilled biologists who have permits should trap tortoises.

Can trapping and **burrow excavation** are methods currently used to remove tortoises from land that has been approved for development. To do this, land owners or developers hire **environmental consultants**. The consultants must study the site and get a **permit** from the U.S. Fish and Wildlife Service (in Alabama, Mississippi, and Louisiana) or from their state regulatory agency (in Florida, Georgia, and South Carolina) to carry out a relocation of the tortoises. The main emphasis of capturing tortoises for **relocation** is to carefully and safely remove them and other protected burrow inhabitants from the **donor** site to a proper **recipient** site.

How do we know you?

What kind of data is collected when we study tortoises?

Each tortoise is given a number. At first it may be temporary; written with permanent markers on duct tape (wrapped completely around the tortoise shell) or painted on with a nontoxic paint.

A permanent form of marking is to drill holes in selected **scutes** or scales. Since these scales are skin and cover living bone, this process is like piercing your ear or nose. To do this, the tortoise must be secured on a cushioned pad to keep it still to be sure that it will not be injured during the drilling. Sometimes a file is used to make a notch in the scale instead of using a drill, but these notches may close up or chip off, making the number hard to read.

To keep records on the tortoise it must be given a number. The number of the tortoise in the drawing to the right is 285. Each time a tortoise is recaptured the number allows us to compare its current weight and condition with past records. This data helps us learn more about a tortoise's life history.

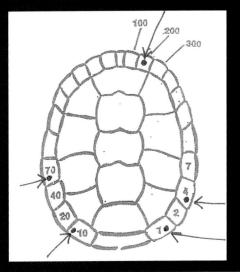

After the tortoise is safely removed from the burrow (by **trapping** or **excavation**) and placed in a numbered bin, it gets a **checkup** very similar to any human visit to the doctor.

Can we take a tortoise's **temperature**? It is not done with a glass thermometer or a probe. A handheld remote sensing digital thermometer is used. We can take the tortoise's temperature without ever touching it.

Then the **data sheet** is completed. The data sheet tells many things, including how far down the tortoise burrow went, whether it curved right or left, and the humidity in the end chamber. It even gives the temperature of the tortoise when it was caught.

TORTOISE BURROW EXCAVATION DATA SHEET

LOCATION _Jones Tract_ (section-township-range) _11-11-16_

HABITAT _Longleaf Pine – Turkey Oak_

DATE _June 16, 2002_ Time to Take _48 minutes_ taken to excavate the burrow.

EXCAVATORS _Ray Ashton , PS Ashton ,_

Burrow No. _216_ Circle (Active) Inactive FWC abandoned

Length _18 ft._ Depth _6.5 ft._ Temp _74°F_

Circle: Left (Right) Straight Spiral Depth of water table _7 ft._

Moisture _damp in_ , Type of Hard pan _limestone_
end chamber→ _82% relative humidity_
Tortoise Present Temp. _82°F_ Other tortoise _none._

Other Vertebrates:
2 Florida mice, S. Hognose

Invertebrates Present and relative abundance:
many mole crickets; unknown gnats at burrow mouth (sample #216A04); beetles (unknown sample #216 A 05–10); gopher ticks (5); 1 snail (unknown sample #216 A 11)

Other Notes:
Sample of feces collected. Burrow recently "cleaned" with much fresh soil at mouth and palate.

How do you measure a tortoise and assess its current health?

First, we **weigh the tortoise** using a spring scale and a plastic grocery bag. The tortoise is not hurt by being in the bag and since most tortoises defecate when weighed, the feces can also be weighed. Using a plastic bag saves lots of time—if we had used a bucket to weigh the tortoise it would have to be washed every time.

Blood is drawn and placed in a special container which is then spun in a centrifuge until the serum (clear) separates. This is used to test for URTD (upper respiratory tract disease). The blood is stored in a freezer for later DNA testing.

The weight, size of the **plastron** (picture 1) and **carapace** (picture 2) can provide important information on the health of the tortoise. If a tortoise has lost weight, it may not be getting access to enough quality **forage** (food). Blood samples may be taken to test for exposure to URTD. The ratio of weight to carapace length can be compared.

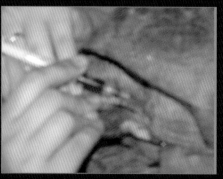

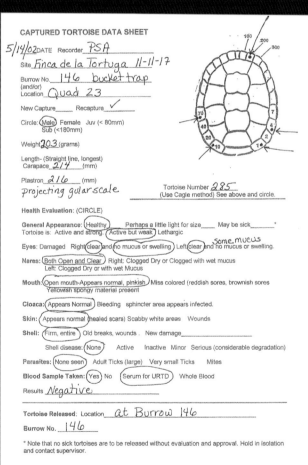

CAPTURED TORTOISE DATA SHEET

5/14/02 DATE Recorder PSA

Site Finca de la Tortuga 11-11-17

Burrow No. 146 bucket trap (and/or)

Location Quad 23

New Capture_____ Recapture ✓

Circle: (Male) Female Juv (< 80mm)
Sub (<180mm)

Weight 203 (grams)

Length- (Straight line, longest)
Carapace 214 (mm)

Plastron 216 (mm)
projecting gular scale

Tortoise Number 285
(Use Cagle method) See above and circle.

Health Evaluation: (CIRCLE)

General Appearance: (Healthy) Perhaps a little light for size_____ May be sick_____ *
Tortoise is: Active and strong. (Active but weak) Lethargic

Eyes: Damaged Right (clear and no mucus or swelling) Left (clear and no mucus or swelling.) some mucus

Nares: (Both Open and Clear) Right: Clogged Dry or Clogged with wet mucus
Left: Clogged Dry or with wet Mucus

Mouth: (Open mouth-Appears normal, pinkish) Miss colored (reddish sores, brownish sores
Yellowish spongy material present

Cloaca: (Appears Normal) Bleeding sphincter area appears infected.

Skin: (Appears normal (healed scars) Scabby white areas Wounds

Shell: (Firm, entire) Old breaks, wounds . New damage_____

Shell disease: (None) Active Inactive Minor Serious (considerable degradation)

Parasites: (None seen) Adult Ticks (large) Very small Ticks Mites

Blood Sample Taken: (Yes) No (Serum for URTD) Whole Blood

Results Negative
_____

Tortoise Released: Location at Burrow 146

Burrow No. 146

* Note that no sick tortoises are to be released without evaluation and approval. Hold in isolation and contact supervisor.

Anytime a tortoise is captured, either as part of a study or for relocation, a data sheet like the one above can be filled out.

IV. Daily Life

How do gopher tortoises meet their needs?
How do they maintain body moisture?

We need to know more about what gopher tortoises do in all seasons and in all weather, throughout the day and night, to manage tortoise habitat and preserves successfully.

How are the daily and seasonal needs of a tortoise met?

(Think about what you do each day.)
A gopher tortoise has to:
- find and maintain shelter – dig a burrow
- maintain body temperature – bask in sun
- maintain body moisture and get water – stay in burrow, drink
- find, eat, and digest food – forage
- eliminate waste from body – excrete feces
- establish home range – one third to 2 acres
- escape predators – slip into burrow or hide
- defend territory and compete for space and mates
- reproduce – courtship, mating, dig nest, lay eggs
- grow and develop – hatchling, juvenile, sub-adult, adult
- recover from injuries or illness
- rest and sleep

The daily life cycle of a tortoise is controlled by the need to maintain body temperature within an acceptable range between 12 and 35 degrees Celsius (55 to 95 degrees Farenheit)—not too hot and not too cold.

Finding and maintaining shelter

You have already learned that burrows are the key to gopher tortoise survival. Gopher tortoises keep their burrows clean and maintain the apron at the burrow mouth so they have a clear view and are also able to slide down in a hurry to escape predators. The burrow mouth acts to funnel sounds downward so the tortoise can hear danger before coming up to the opening, where it is vulnerable.

Maintaining body temperature

The sandy apron serves as a safe basking area where the ectothermic (cold-blooded) tortoise can sit in the sun and raise its body temperature in order to move and digest food properly.

path of rain water

Tortoise drinking

Maintaining body moisture

You are never too young to discover something new in science. The authors' 12-year-old son, Kevin, was the first to see that in heavy rains, some gopher tortoises come up to drink at the mouth of their burrow where water is running off the mound and backside of the burrow into the burrow mouth. By scraping with and then positioning one front foot, the tortoise creates a channel and then it puts its head down to suck up a bellyful of water in twenty seconds.

Tortoises live in dry sandy areas where water soaks in rapidly, so this is an important strategy for getting water. They may go to drink or soak in temporary ponds or forage in marshes, and they can swim. They have been seen eating leaves heavy with rain or dew. The end chamber of their burrow is at the water table so the humidity there is higher than in the hot sun of their sandhills habitat. One function of their scaly skin is to help prevent water loss in dry climates.

How do you find food, eat, and eliminate wastes?

Finding, selecting, eating, and digesting food

- Gopher tortoises are like cows with shells. They eat a lot of bulk (grasses and leaves), which takes up a lot of the time they spend foraging.
- We still don't know how they locate forage that is not in the immediate area of the burrow. They use sight and smell to check out plants before tasting and eating them.
- They definitely remember the presence of favorite plants and return to them again and again. Evidence shows they select specific plants or plant parts at different times, perhaps to meet specific metabolic needs.
- They may come out to eat every day or, when the weather is mild and they require more time for digestion, only once every 2 to 3 days.
- During very warm to hot periods when plants are actively growing and flowers and fruits are plentiful, they may forage 2 or 3 times a day for 20 minutes to 2 hours and then retreat to their burrow or the shade of trees or shrubs to cool down and digest their food.
- Tortoises depend on a varied and plentiful microfauna (bacteria, round worms) in their intestines to aid in digestion of tough plant materials.

If a winter day is warm enough, the tortoise may come up to the burrow mouth to bask in the sun. Once it warms up it will forage.

Eliminating waste from the body

Tortoises usually defecate (excrete feces) **while on the move**, sometimes leaving a trail of one or two blobs of semi-moist feces in their path. The feces contain the things they did not digest, like seeds and the less digestible cellulose that makes up the stems and leaves of grasses and herbs. If tortoises are **attacked** they may also excrete feces and liquid as a response to stress and to surprise the attacker.

Which direction was this tortoise going when it released this feces?

(from right to left)

How do we know what you eat?

How do biologists determine forage species and availability?

Biologists who study plants are called **botanists**, and they work with herpetologists to understand not only how tortoises eat but also on what, when, and where they forage. They watch and photograph or film tortoises foraging, making note of what species and parts they eat throughout the seasons. They also analyze the tortoise feces for undigested plant parts. These studies have to be done in all the different habitats throughout the tortoise's range. Botanists measure the diversity of grasses and herbaceous species available to the tortoise in each habitat. The data collected on all these plants must be entered into a computer and analyzed to help with future management of the forage. The quality and quantity of forage available in a habitat must be monitored regularly to determine what management practices may be required. For example, if the tree canopy is shading out grasses, then prescribed burning may be needed.

A series of transects should be done to assess the quality of the forage for tortoises to eat. The plant species inside each .25 by .25 meter quadrant (like the square shown in the photo to the left) are recorded each time the quadrant is placed at meter marks along a 50- or 100- meter transect. The total number of transects to be done depends upon the habitat and diversity.

MAP OF PLANT COMMUNITIES FOR RECIPIENT SITE

LEGEND
MARSH
LIVE OAK HAMMOCK
TURKEY OAK SCRUB
LONG LEAF PINE
ROSEMARY SCRUB
PLANTED SLASH PINE
OLD PASTURE
WAX MYRTLE-OAK

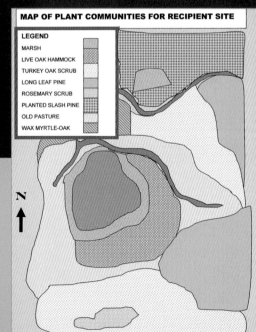

N

From the data collected during a botanical survey, from aerial maps, and from transects, a map of plant communities can be drawn.

HANDBOOK OF GOPHER TORTOISE MANAGEMENT AND CONSERVATION

DATA SHEET   Air Temp. 85°F   Transect # 2A03   S→N   Ashton, Ashton & Associates, Inc.   DATE 7/5/03   STAFF PSA, REA, M?

GOPHER TORTOISE FORAGE DATA SHEET
HERBACEOUS BELT TRANSECT: GROUND COVER QUADRATS
.25 sq. meter quadrats in 50 meter long and .5 meter wide belt transect

QUADRAT #	01	02	03	04	05	06	07	08	09	10
Max. Vegetation Height (in cm)	2cm	22cm	17cm	7cm	4cm	30cm	12cm	24cm	0cm	8cm
Water level (in cm) / Soil Moisture	0	0	0	0	0	0	0	0	0	.3cm	.1cm
SPECIES # OR NAME or UNKNOWN #										
Wiregrass	4	X	2	4	2		6	4		
Unknown grass 6/4/03			X	1	X		1	X		
Smilax a.	X	1		2	2		2			2
Milk pea	X	1	1						X	2
Bracken fern	2	4	2			2	5	1	X	
Pawpaw Asi.			1	1		1				
Winged Sumac	2					X		2		
Bahia		1								
Black Root			X	1		X		1		
Reindeer Lichen	2	1			X	X				
Long-Leaf Pine								3		
Rosemary			X							
Turkey Oak	1		1				X			
Live Oak					2	1				
Bluejack Oak										
Persimmon										
Goldenrod	X				1					
Deer's Tongue		X					X			
Dead leaves/ Lichens	X		X	X	1	2	X		6	4

Cover Classes   Range of Cover   Comments:

X - covers less than 1%   Gopher apple in fruit (just off transect)
1 - covers 1% to 5%   Sensitive plant in flower west of transect
2 - covers 5% to 25%   Standing puddles after yesterday's rain
3 - covers 25% to 50%   Saw palmetto to east of transect
4 - covers 51% to 75%
5 - covers 75% to 95%
6 - covers 95% to 100%

Prepared by
Ray E. Ashton, Jr. and Patricia S. Ashton   5 of 14

This data sheet is used for recording the plants found during a survey of potential tortoise forage. The data would be entered into a computer and analyzed.

What plants do you seek?

Which plant do you want to nibble?

Tortoises seek out many different plants, using their eyesight and their sense of smell. You can observe a tortoise put its nose to the plant and inhale before taking a bite. Plants produce different chemical substances in leaves, stems, fruits, and flowers as they progress through their life cycle. Tortoises appear to be able to detect these chemical changes. When some plants are repeatedly grazed they produce toxic or distasteful chemicals and may be avoided. Injured plants produce fungicides or antibiotics at the site of the wound. When grasses are repeatedly grazed they produce more proteins. Tortoises may select plant species specifically for these chemicals in addition to the carbohydrates and proteins they contain. In a sense they are practicing herbal medicine.

1. Blackberry
2. Pepper grass and Paspalum
3. Gopher apple
4. Bracken fern
5. Mexican clover
6. Blueberry

What plants do you like?

From which plant families do tortoises like to eat?

Some of the most common plant families containing plants tortoises like to eat are listed below in the order of most commonly eaten to less frequently selected. Which of these plant families have foods that you eat?

Seagrape

Milk pea

Smilax

Stinging nettle

Wild grape

Paspalum grass

Poison ivy

Scorpiontail

Beautyberry

FAMILY	COMMON PLANTS EATEN FROM FAMILY
GRASS	almost all species of grasses; love Paspalum, broadleafed grasses
ASTER	chaffhead, bidens, wild lettuce, asters, hawkweed, ragweed, daisies
PEA/BEAN	milk pea, clover, sandweed, vetch, butterfly pea, cow pea
SPURGE	beach spurge, 3-seeded mercury, stinging nettle, phyllanthus
GOOSEFOOT	lamb's quarters, sea blite, seabeach orach, saltbush, glasswort
VERVAIN	lantana, verbena, blue porterweed, match heads, beautyberry
AMARANTH	chaff flower, pigweed, samphire, alternanthera, alligatorweed
MUSTARD	peppergrass, wild radish, shepard's purse, sea rocket
ROSE	blackberry, loquat
GRAPE	wild grape, fox grape, summer grape, Virginia creeper
NIGHTSHADE	ground cherry, petunia, garden egg plant, tomatoes, peppers
HEATH	blueberry, huckleberry, fetterbush, rusty lyonia, doghobble
SUMAC	poison ivy, Brazilian pepper, winged sumac
MADDER	Mexican clover, poor Joe or diodia, buttonwood, beach creeper
BORAGE	scorpion tail or heliotrope
COCO PLUM	coco plum, gopher apple
BUCKWHEAT	seagrape, pigeon plum, wild buckwheat, jointweed, dock
MINT	henbit, heal-all, betony, coleus, lyre-leafed sage, germander
SMILAX	smilax, greenbriar, catbriar, sarsaparilla
CACTUS	prickly pear cactus

What is good forage for you?

How can we recognize suitable or potential tortoise forage?

Tortoises find suitable forage plants in healthy coastal, uplands, clay hills, and flatwoods habitats with good biodiversity. Tortoises obtain bulk (largely indigestible plant fiber) by eating lots and lots of broad-leafed grasses and some wire grasses. In this way, they are like cows munching mouthfuls of pasture grass. Selectively eating particular plants or parts of plants is similar to humans taking medicines or vitamins to stay healthy. For this reason, it is important that tortoises have a large diversity of plant species available. Tortoises are known to eat 300 to 400 different species of plants.

Knowing how to recognize potential forage species and identify the level of species diversity is very important. **Identification of forage** and determination of the quality of forage or potential for forage with proper management is vital.

Signs of good forage:

- Plenty of broad-leafed grasses
- Wiregrasses with open space
- Diversity of plant species
- Sunny, unshaded, open
- Good seed source and seed bank for continued diversity
- Any trees are widely spaced
- Good drainage
- Some fruiting bushes / trees
- Plenty of flowering / weedy herbaceous species
- Ground cover is not too dense
- Open ground for reseeding

Butterfly pea

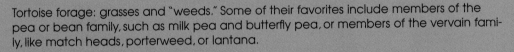

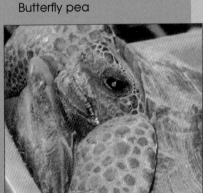

Tortoise forage: grasses and "weeds." Some of their favorites include members of the pea or bean family, such as milk pea and butterfly pea, or members of the vervain family, like match heads, porterweed, or lantana.

Herbaceous "weeds" are really wildflowers that produce seeds and fruits eaten by many birds and insects as well as by gopher tortoises. In different seasons tortoises select different plant parts like leaves, stems, flowers, fruits, seeds, seed pods, and sometimes roots.

Tortoises do not have teeth. They have a bony beak that cuts plants just like a pair of scissors. They also use their tongue to help move the plants into their mouth and down their throat. Tortoises have certain bacteria and roundworms in their intestines that help digest the **cellulose** (fiber) in plants. Thus more nutrients are obtained. Tortoises use their senses of sight and smell to search out important plants and then select specific plants and plant parts to provide needed nutrients. Nutrients in plants depend on the fertility or nutrient levels in the soils. In sandy soils, nutrients are easily lost.

Do you farm to produce the plants you like to eat? How?

What do farmers do that tortoises can also do to help plants grow?

Do tortoises farm? Our research says yes, in a way of thinking, they do help to create the conditions for the plants they like to eat. In addition to bringing up fertile soil, tortoises roam widely, feeding on their favorite plants and bringing the seeds back in their feces. Some of these seeds may end up in a suitable place to **germinate** (break out of the seed coat and start to grow using the energy stored in the seed). Tortoises repeatedly graze the same grass plants, which interrupts the reproductive cycle of these plants and causes them to put out new tender growth to replace what they lost. This benefits the tortoise, providing more nutritional forage. Tortoises weed their garden by ripping some weed species out by the roots and eating them, which opens space for other useful seedlings.

Wow. That's a lot of work to move yards and yards of sand to keep the burrow open and also create a perfect "seed bed" for new, tender and tasty young plants. The tortoise often rips these plants out by the roots and eats the whole thing. In other cases, the tortoise may simply nip off a leaf or two one day, and then a few days later, remove another leaf from the same plant.

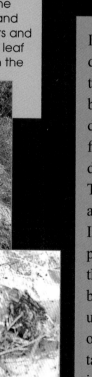

Tortoise feces with leaves and seeds.

In sandy areas, water carries nutrients down until they hit a hardpan or water table. The tortoise tends its garden by bringing up soil rich in nutrients from deep underground and spreading it out from the burrow just as a farmer or gardener would plow and fertilize the land. This fresh sand also provides an open area for seeds to germinate and grow. In a pasture of grass where herbaceous plants have a hard time competing with the tightly packed grasses, the tortoise, both by burrowing and feeding, opens up the ground cover (as shown in photo of pasture above) to allow herbaceous tasty weedy forage species to grow and increase the biodiversity.

When do you forage?

When can you or a land manager observe tortoises foraging?

Tortoises are herbivorous and they forage (graze) on plant materials just as cows, rabbits, and deer do. They may eat a lot of one plant like grass near their burrow or they may walk a long way, over 1000 meters (3500 feet), to choose a particular part (a flower, fruit, or leaf) of a certain plant, such as their favorite, Mexican clover. Tortoises have enemies to avoid, and they can get too hot or too cold. They change the time of day and the length of time they come out of their burrow in response to these dangers. Unless you know when and where to look for a tortoise feeding you might never see anything but their tracks, pushed-down vegetation where they walked, or the grass bitten off as evidence of their foraging. You have to sit quietly and watch or the tortoise will run back to its burrow. Can you see something a tortoise may have eaten?

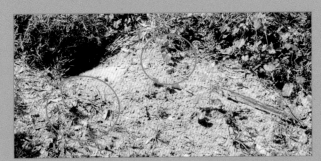

Young herbs and tender grape leaves

Nutgrass or sedge

Tortoises forage at different times in different seasons. They begin to forage when the temperature is warm enough but not too hot. This graph of their activity times can help you know when to look for a tortoise foraging. They generally forage for 20 minutes to 2 hours at a time. A high foraging level means they are likely to be out eating at that time. A low foraging level means the tortoises are rarely out foraging at that time.

Summer ——————

Fall ——————

Winter ——————

Spring ——————

Foraging Level	Sunrise	Mid-AM	Mid-Day	Mid-PM	Sunset
High					
Medium					
Low					
None					

Where can you find and observe tortoises foraging?

Even after you know the general area where tortoises are feeding, it takes lots of patience to find and photograph or video gopher tortoises eating. If you select the correct time of day based on the temperature, humidity, and season (refer to graph on previous page) and if you learn to move quietly and slowly in the tortoise's habitat, then you might get to see a tortoise actually feeding, instead of just traveling from one place to another. Tortoises can feel vibrations in the ground and may hear very low frequency sounds, which travel long distances. They know you are coming before you see them. If you are able to recognize places tortoises have been foraging, then you can wait for the tortoise to come out and feed. How do you recognize places where tortoises have been feeding? Look for feeding trails that lead from the burrow to good foraging areas. In sandy areas, tracks are easy to follow. Also look for feces; the pointed part shows the direction of travel (see photo on page 31). Bites that have been taken out of grasses, tender cactus pads, stems, leaves, or ripe gopher apple fruits are also evidence that a tortoise has been there.

Juvenile seeking food along a feeding trail from burrow

We watched a tortoise eat off each flowering segment of this Mexican clover plant.

The close-up of Carphephorus shows repeated tortoise bites.

This photo shows a feeding trail leading to a palmetto with flowers (a tortoise favorite), young ferns, Carphephorus and gopher apple grow nearby and the leaves show signs of grazing by the tortoise. Tortoise feces on the trail had gopher apple seeds and blueberry leaves in it.

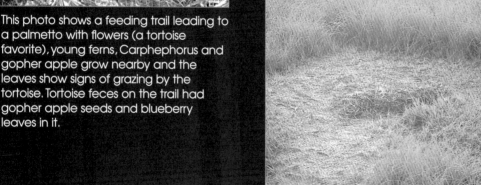

This tortoise burrow in a grassy field shows clearly the area where the tortoise grazed the grass and ate some herbs— roots and all.

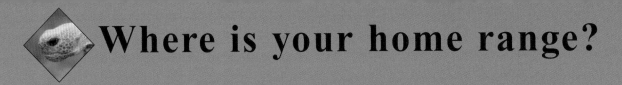

Where is your home range?

How far do you travel from your home each day?

A tortoise's life centers around its burrows and its forage areas. Your "home range" centers around your house and school and pizza place and friends' houses. These are places you visit regularly. The gopher tortoise may have one to three burrows in an area where it spends most of its time. This area is called the tortoise's **home range** and it can be less than one third of an acre or more than two acres, depending on the type and quality of the habitat. The home range for a tortoise is mostly defined by its foraging areas. Other tortoises also will live clustered near those good foraging areas, and so we say all these tortoises together make a **pod**. With the changing seasons or with drought, the habitat and nature of the forage for the tortoise may change. Just as you might visit grandma at the beach for the summer, the tortoise may travel (2 to 5 miles) and take up temporary residence in an existing burrow or dig a new burrow. The tortoise may visit for a period of time or stay and socialize with members of a new pod and become a permanent resident. Perhaps this change in home range is stimulated by the "smell" of a particular fruit or food on the wind, leading the tortoise to find it in a new forage area and establish a new home base. After a period of time, the tortoise may return to its original home range and pod and even to its original burrow.

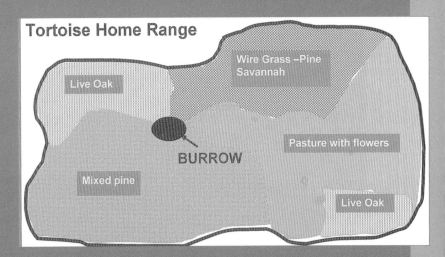

Tortoise Home Range

Wire Grass –Pine Savannah

Live Oak

Pasture with flowers

BURROW

Mixed pine

Live Oak

If a tortoise's home range begins to change—too many saplings grow into mature trees and shade the once-open savannah or a river shifts its course and the dry upland is flooded—then these changes will affect the tortoise's forage. Changes in the composition (kinds of plants) and quantity of forage can cause a tortoise to move to a new home range. No one knows if the tortoises leave one by one to find new home ranges or whether they can "trail" or follow each other to a new location.

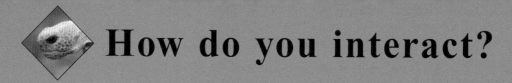
What are some defensive and social behaviors exhibited by gopher tortoises?

Escape predators. Tortoises dive into their burrow or depend upon their shell and tough scales for protection. They also depend on camouflage to escape the notice of predators. They are vulnerable as hatchlings, juveniles, and subadults to predators from above the burrow such as crows, hawks or owls. Predators like raccoons, opossums, foxes, dogs, or coyotes can enter the burrow or lie in wait. These predators can eat the hatchlings or juveniles and may also eat the eggs from the nest. The hatchlings and juveniles are good at hiding under grass clumps and vegetation.

Defend territory and compete. Male-to-male aggression usually involves a lot of head bobbing, ramming and pushing, and defecating. One tortoise may be able to use its gular to flip the other, leaving it in a vulnerable position if it is not strong enough to turn back over. Predators or the hot sun may kill a tortoise left on its back. Males may encounter each other while foraging or when visiting female burrows in preparation for courtship and mating. A strong male can run a competitor out of his area and keep the females to himself.

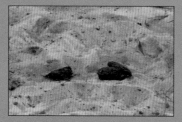

Fresh tortoise feces left behind after the aggressive encounter above.

Tortoises know the area around their burrow very well and are able to slip into the shade or slide into the shadows of trees or shrubby ground cover all along the paths and trails to their burrow. The dark-colored, mottled shell acts as **camouflage** in the vegetation.

How can we learn about your social activities?

What kinds of social behaviors do we observe in tortoises?

Studies of many different species of tortoises show a variety of social interactions such as head bobbing, nose touching, following each other (trailing), and direct aggression like ramming. Gopher tortoises are a little anti-social in that they do not feed in groups, they do not generally share burrows or travel in groups, and they are somewhat aggressive to other tortoises entering their immediate area. They do, however, seem to have burrows grouped in pods probably due to the presence of good forage and good burrowing soils in that area. Studies have shown that the same females have maintained burrows for years in the same pod. Females don't usually tolerate other females in the same burrow but in spring a male may be found in a female's burrow with the female.

Special equipment, like the antenna and receiver (photo above, left), is used to track the radio signal from a transmitter placed on the tortoise's shell with epoxy (photo above, right). These techniques can help us learn more about how tortoises move in their home range and can give us clues about how they interact with each other socially.

This tortoise behavior researcher in this picture sat for hours in a tree stand observing tortoise behaviors. The authors have also followed gopher tortoises and video recorded their behavior for analysis. Many tortoise species demonstrate social interactions such as head bobbing, trailing, sniffing, nose touching, and ramming.

Doing behavioral research is very tiring. It requires long hours of just watching and waiting for the tortoises to come out or to actually do something. Tortoises live in areas where they are often hidden by vegetation and you must watch for every little movement to reveal their presence.

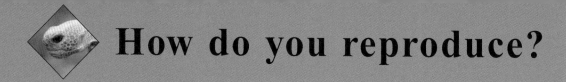

How do tortoises court, mate, dig a nest, lay eggs, hatch, and grow?

The male tortoise usually travels to various burrows occupied by females within his territory. Mating occurs in spring (usually April; the exact time depends upon the latitude). The male will follow the female around when she comes out of the burrow to forage. He will bob his head up and down and trail behind her and then cut in front of her to try to wipe his leg barb covered in **pheromones** near her nose. Or he may rub her with his chin, which has scent glands. We don't know yet if the low frequency sounds tortoises make play any role in courtship or mating.

The female usually digs a nest 15 to 30 days after mating if she has had sufficient nutritional forage available to be able to make eggs. She digs a nest, usually in or near the burrow apron, and deposits 5–7 round eggs. If her burrow is under a palmetto or at the shaded edge of the woods, she may nest nearby in a sandy area in the sun. The eggs develop in the sand, warmed by the sun, and usually hatch in 80–100 days. Hatchling tortoises may take refuge in inactive adult burrows. They have been observed eating adult feces as well as insects and tender forage plants. Eventually they make or find their own burrow. The hatchling's yellow and brown splotched scales help them to be well camouflaged in dry leaves and grasses and help them meld into the shadows. In about 4 years they darken and remain juveniles for about 6-10 years, depending upon how much forage there is and how fast they grow. Between 10 and 20 years old they are classed (by size) as subadults. They become sexually mature (as determined by size) and able to reproduce at about 18–25 years old and then may live 60 years or more.

Once the female is ready to mate, the male mounts her from behind. His concave plastron helps him balance on her shell. Sometimes he taps the top of her shell which may help to keep her still during **copulation**. His long, bluish-colored penis enters the opening (**cloaca**) under the female's tail. Males may make low, audible sounds during the exertion of copulating. Copulation may last 10-20 minutes. If the female is unreceptive or frightened, she may lift up and push the male over on his back.

It's hard to photograph tortoises mating in the wild. You have to follow them at the correct time of year, be patient, and be very, very lucky.

Burrow mouth

Nest mouth before covered by the tortoise

Human dug excavation to get to the nest cavity and the eggs.

The record number of gopher tortoise eggs found in one nest was about 25.

A hatchling under 1 year old at an inactive adult burrow mouth.

What if you get hurt or sick?

Should I take a sick or hurt gopher tortoise to a veterinarian?

Tortoises use their burrows for rest and for recovering from injury or illness. Tortoises get hit by cars, stepped on by cows, run over by farm or land clearing machinery, and attacked by dogs. If you find an injured tortoise, what should you do to best help it survive? In most cases, the best choice is to leave the tortoise alone or to place it at the mouth of the nearest burrow. Stress (from handling, treating, or moving the tortoise) can slow or prevent recovery.

We now have many examples of how injured tortoises that are simply allowed to return to their own burrow and are not interfered with are found again months later healed and healthy.

Gopher tortoises in the wild depend on round worms and microfauna in their intestines to help digest the tough vegetation they eat. A healthy tortoises' intestines are like a whole ecosystem. Treatment with antibiotics and de-worming medications may do more harm than good. Sometimes help hurts. In a coastal county a sign was needed to remind residents not to "return" these dry land tortoises to the ocean. Signs have also been used to remind people to drive slowly in areas where tortoises cross roads and highways.

How can I tell if the tortoise is sick?

Sick tortoises may have nasal discharge, "gummy" eyes, and be very light in weight for their size. Keeping a sick tortoise in captivity increases its stress level and is more likely to prevent a recovery. Upper Respiratory Tract Disease (URTD) is one of many illnesses tortoises can get (just as you get the flu, colds and infections). Sick or injured tortoises seem to head for their burrow and may remain down in the burrow for an extended period. Very ill gopher tortoises have been found in a lethargic state at the mouth of their burrow. Tortoises can die from URTD or other illnesses, but many recover. Injured tortoises that are able to move, but with severely cracked and bleeding shells, have been returned to the nearest burrow and allowed to go down to their end chamber. Then they have been found again 6-9 months later feeding and apparently healthy with the cracked shell in the process of healing. Tortoises appear to go into a resting state in the burrow while they are healing. In most cases it is best to leave the tortoise alone and not cause further stress.

V. Where the Gopher Tortoise Lives

Where do you go in a fire?

Are forest fires a danger to tortoises? Why do they live in fire-maintained habitats?

Gopher tortoises live in habitats that have many types of grasses and **herbaceous** plant species to eat. There are trees but not so many as to shade out the plants on the ground. Fire is the reason why the trees are not too dense. Fire burns these **savannahs** (grasslands with scattered trees) every few years. As long as fire comes often enough the trees will be thinned out by the fire and it will not burn too hot. The remaining widely spaced trees result in a **canopy** (open tree cover) that allows sunlight to reach the herbs and grasses on the ground. If fire is kept out of these savannahs, too many trees and bushes will grow. A closed canopy shades out and kills many forage plants. Too much leaf litter (dead leaves) and dead branches can build up on the ground and act as fuel for a hot, deadly wildfire.

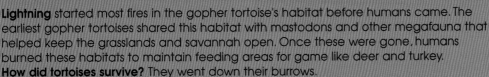

Lightning started most fires in the gopher tortoise's habitat before humans came. The earliest gopher tortoises shared this habitat with mastodons and other megafauna that helped keep the grasslands and savannah open. Once these were gone, humans burned these habitats to maintain feeding areas for game like deer and turkey.
How did tortoises survive? They went down their burrows.

Longleaf pine uplands habitat

Gopher tortoises go into their burrows where they are protected from the heat and smoke. They aren't the only animals that use the burrows when there is a fire. Other species also make use of the tortoise burrow as an adaptation to life in these habitats maintained by frequent fires. When hot, uncontrolled wildfires rush through a habitat, tortoises and other wildlife may be caught and burned. Tortoises have been observed avoiding the fire line of a normal, slow-moving fire.

How does fire help keep habitats healthy and help maintain forage plants?

Plants chosen as forage by tortoises are genetically adapted to well-drained soils, sunlight, and periodic fires.

After a fire, nutrients are returned to the soil and the ground is ready for seeds to grow—both seeds lying dormant in the soil **(seed bank)** and seeds brought in on the wind or by animals from surrounding unburned areas **(seed source)**. Some plants will survive and others will die, depending on the season when the fire burns and on how hot it burns. Wiregrass, longleaf pine, and other plant species designed to survive fire have protected or underground parts from which new growth emerges. Wiregrass (photo below) shows the first green shoots within days of the fire, along with smilax, bracken fern, and broad-leafed grasses.

The large healthy trees still live unless it was a very hot fire. Even these trees usually lose most of their leaves in the weeks after a burn. The leaf fall also helps add nutrients and retain moisture in the soil. Opening the tree canopy so the sun hits open ground to enhance plant growth is the most important end result of fire. If there has been rain, then within a week or two of a burn new sprouts will appear and deer and tortoises will take advantage of the tender young shoots of wiregrass, broad-leafed grasses, ferns, palmetto, and a great variety of wildflowers. This new growth is rich in nutrients and proteins, making high quality forage for tortoises and other wildlife.

1 day after burn

1 week after burn

new sprouts of wiregrass and ferns

2 weeks after burn

VI. How We Help the Gopher Tortoise

Why do we manage your habitat?

How can humans and tortoises share the same habitats?

New roads and new developments are moving into the habitats of the Southeastern states that the gopher tortoise also calls home. In Florida, where over 1000 new residents may arrive daily, wild habitats are rapidly becoming housing developments. Upland habitats are naturally fire-maintained, but people, houses, and fire do not easily mix. Without regular fires these habitats become overgrown, and the threat of wildfire increases. Without fire the native vegetation that tortoises, deer, turkey, and other wildlife depend on for food is shaded out. **Prescribed burning** is an important management tool to protect both human and wildlife habitats. The best way for humans, tortoises, and other wildlife to coexist is to have well-planned **habitat management.** Educating everyone on why fire is an important tool for habitat management is one way to help gopher tortoises. Another way is to support enforcement of laws and regulations permitting controlled burning in upland habitats near development.

Most (but not all) management practices of forestry, farming, ranching, wildlife management areas, county parks, and recreational areas can be compatible with the needs of native wildlife, including the gopher tortoise and its burrow associates.

What happens to tortoises and other wildlife when people move into uplands?

More people than ever are living on earth and moving into areas where there were once only trees, flowers, and wildlife. Cities, schools, stores, golf courses, and roads now cover the lands that were home to gopher tortoises, deer, turkey, and great longleaf pine trees. Many city parks are groomed with exotic grasses, trees, and shrubs alien to native wildlife and are sprayed with pesticides that kill native species. In many parts of the Southeast the only areas left for wildlife are roadsides, farms, ranches, forestry lands, undeveloped properties, and properties owned by conservation organizations or various government agencies.

Everyday some of the remaining undeveloped lands are cleared and turned into new housing developments, roads, businesses, and shopping centers.

Conservationists and some governmental agencies are trying to find ways to save tortoises and all of the other wildlife in our uplands while still allowing humans to continue to move on to these uplands, build houses, and also enjoy the environment. We need good **conservation plans** for lands where gopher tortoises and wildlife still survive. A good conservation plan takes all the information we know about tortoises and other wildlife and tells land managers the best ways to care for the properties and the wildlife that depends on those habitats.

Where will the tortoises go?
In central Florida this roadside sign uses a tortoise to advertise uplands for sale for building houses or businesses.

As lands are developed, tortoises that are not killed can become isolated in remnants of vegetation along roadsides or in yards or city parks. These lone animals cannot find mates and usually die a slow death. They may be killed by cars or poisoned by pesticides. Humanitarian relocations can move these individuals to preserves where they may not contribute to the preservation of the species, but they do live out their lives (60 years or more) and perhaps serve an educational purpose to remind humans that tortoises still need properly managed **habitat.**

What can landowners do to live their own lives and still protect habitat?

In spite of regulations protecting tortoises, there are far fewer tortoises today than just 25 years ago. We have no way to protect all the gopher tortoises that are still alive today. As their habitat is taken on a daily basis for human use, there are fewer and fewer places for them. Mitigation parks, state and national parks and wildlife refuges, conservation lands, and local parks purchased for habitat protection all can help, but they cannot support all the tortoises that are being displaced daily. Landowners with ranches, farms, forests, and large properties are encouraged to manage that land so tortoises and other wildlife can live in harmony with the human uses of the land. Permanent **conservation easements** that protect the land from development can be purchased from landowners by the state or local governments. In addition to a cash payment for the easement, the landowner can receive tax incentives to manage the land properly for wildlife. Landowners can obtain from state and federal conservation agencies **safe harbor agreements** to avoid penalties for doing a good job in protecting and increasing protected species of wildlife on their properties.

Will the sun set forever on the characteristic silhouette of the longleaf pine found in upland habitats? Faster-growing pine species are being planted in close rows on cleared uplands for profit and to maintain tax breaks for the landowner. These planted pines shade out tortoise forage and turn the forest floor into a desert covered in pine needles. Few creatures can find food in these "pine deserts."

Uplands are cleared to plant pines.

No tortoises and little wildlife survive in this planted pine desert.

Where do the gopher tortoises go when humans move in?

When humans want to move in, tortoises can be

1) **protected** on that same site
2) **relocated** to a new site
3) **"taken"** by permit, meaning that they and their burrows may be destroyed

What determines which of the three above actions will be taken?

Decisions are usually made based on regulations and on what is best for the finances and public relations of the developer or landowner.

All three possibilities are available to developers under the state and federal rules for tortoises that test negative for exposure to URTD. In this case decisions may be made based on cost, goals for use of the site, public relations potential, and, often of least concern, the conservation possibilities.

Do you know what the regulations on moving or protecting tortoises are in your county and state?

Under the current rules tortoises that test positive for URTD cannot be moved from the site. When this occurs the developer and the agency can decide whether an on-site preserve is appropriate (see next page) or they may choose to pay into a **mitigation bank** (see page 54) for the loss of the tortoise population on-site.

Relocation of tortoises from a construction site requires a **permit** from the agency overseeing tortoises in that specific area (see appendix).

The process of applying for a permit, designing an on-site or off-site preserve, or creating a mitigation plan should be done by a professional biologist (or a consultant who is a trained biologist) with experience working with gopher tortoises and with management and monitoring of tortoise habitat.

The conservation of the gopher tortoise as a species requires that scientists and regulators plan to protect forever large groups or populations of gopher tortoises in different places. Protecting one tortoise all alone on a piece of property or keeping one or two tortoises in a "zoo" cannot preserve the species over a long period of time. This must be taken into account in all three choices covered in the next three pages.

Choice #1– An on-site preserve
How do we make and take care of an on-site preserve?

Sometimes the landowner or developer is able to set aside part of the property being developed as an on-site preserve rather than move all the animals off site to a recipient location or pay into a mitigation bank and destroy all the animals living there. This is only good for the tortoise if the on-site preserve is large enough, with quality habitat, and if there is a management plan and a monitoring plan in place with the money, expertise, and dedication to carry them out in **perpetuity.**

Usually, after careful planning and negotiations with the agency in charge of permitting, a large area of suitable habitat for gopher tortoises, burrowing owls, scrub jays, kestrels, or other protected species is set aside and properly managed in perpetuity. The home owners or businesses that will occupy the rest of the development site often find these preserves of great benefit. They provide natural green space and attract birds in addition to providing a new home site for tortoises relocated there from the part of the property being used by humans. Sometimes these on-site preserves can also serve as nature parks with walkways and controlled access for local residents.

Florida has a number of successful on-site preserves. This is the on-site preserve at Celebration, Florida.

Gopher tortoise on-site preserve at The Villages of Lady Lake, Florida

The authors worked on the on-site tortoise, kestrel, and burrowing owl preserves at the Villages of Lady Lake where education of the residents was an important aspect of long-term protection for the gopher tortoise and other species. An on-site preserve at Disney's Celebration provides nature paths and informational signs. Homeowners associations and GTCI volunteers have shown they can successfully manage and protect tortoises in developments approaching "build out." When a few lots are left and all the tortoises have burrows on them, moving tortoises is a nightmare for the new homeowner and builders. GTCI volunteers help make sure these tortoises are relocated properly and not just "bulldozed."

Trained GTCI volunteers move tortoises to an on-site preserve in Sugarmill Woods, Citrus County, Florida.

Choice #2– An off-site preserve
How do you make and take care of an off-site relocation preserve?

The first obligation of an off-site relocation preserve is to maintain the quality of the habitat for the original and relocated tortoise populations. All existing tortoise burrows are mapped, numbered, and marked with metal stakes.

Longleaf pine – turkey oak sandhills habitat with wiregrass and a diverse herbaceous ground cover is perfect for a gopher tortoise preserve of over 100 acres called *Finca de la Tortuga* (The Tortoise's Farm)–Ashton Biological Preserve. After proper management including burning, regular monitoring of tortoise populations and vegetation, and exotics eradication, this preserve has become an example of a functional, well-managed off-site relocation preserve. Relocated tortoises are periodically recaptured to monitor their behavior and health since their relocation.

Most of the properties around Ashton Biological Preserve have now been surveyed and are being managed as part of the overall habitat for gopher tortoises and other protected species.

A long-term **habitat monitoring and management plan** helps keep the preserve on track. Private and public off-site preserves are being created throughout Florida and the southeastern U.S., but many more are needed. Funding is also needed for continued monitoring and management. Tortoises may be relocated to these preserves as a result of a **humanitarian** relocation (done to save one or a few tortoises) or as part of a **conservation** relocation of a viable population of tortoises.

Tortoise reserves are those that the owners or managers agree to manage for tortoises along with other uses.

Choice #3– "Taken"
What happens to the tortoises in a "take"?
What is a mitigation bank?

The term tortoise **"take"** sounds harmless enough, but what does it really mean for the tortoise? When a consultant for the developer or land owner applies for a **take permit** and it is approved, then the land owner or developer pays into the **mitigation bank** – a fund used to purchase **mitigation parks.** This allows them to do whatever is necessary to clear and build and landscape on their property. This likely means that they can cover or collapse tortoise burrows. Why then is this a possible choice? Because if done correctly, mitigation banks and parks can help with true **conservation** of the gopher tortoise as a **species**.

Choice # 3 – "taken" decisions have **consequences** for resident gopher tortoises

This is a site being cleared. A tortoise was found crushed in tracks of heavy machinery. Other tortoises are trapped or entombed in their burrows all over the site

The Conservation of the Gopher Tortoise as a Species

True conservation of the species means that **viable** populations of gopher tortoises of sufficient **genetic diversity** must be maintained in suitable, protected, diverse, and well-managed habitats. **Mitigation parks** funded by **mitigation banks** can make this happen.

A viable population—a large group of males and females of all ages (but not all too closely related) including breeding adults and juveniles—must be preserved for gopher tortoises to continue as a species. Mitigation parks need to be very large pieces of suitable property with plenty of tortoise habitat and forage and diverse populations of healthy gopher tortoises. These populations may be augmented by tortoises removed from other sites to further benefit the species as a whole. In theory this is what happens when a "take" permit is approved. The term **mitigation** means the permit applicant has paid money to make up for the actions of "taking" the protected gopher tortoises and their burrows on the project property.

How are tortoises successfully relocated to a preserve?

The methods described here are designed to create a successful **relocation** of healthy tortoises and are based on what we have learned from experience; they may or may not be related to the requirements of a particular agency. Requirements vary by agency and location.

Basic steps for a successful tortoise relocation

1) Evaluate carrying capacity of recipient site, approximately 2–4 tortoises per acre.

2) If needed, conduct management (such as burning) on recipient site at least 3 months prior to relocation.

3) Establish a permanent monitoring and management program for the recipient site.

4) Install either permanent fencing around the entire recipient site or temporary fencing around the specific relocation site.

5) Ensure appropriate removal and care of tortoises from donor site including proper marking and data collection by trained staff.

6) Transport tortoises properly and immediately in suitable containers to the recipient site. Containers should be closed and dark with only 1 or 2 tortoises (from the same pod) in a container.

7) If conditions have been dry, soak tortoises in tepid water for at least an hour to rehydrate them prior to release.

8) Release of the tortoises should be done prior to noon to allow them time to orient themselves before dark.

9) Tortoises should be monitored daily for the first week or until all tortoises have successfully found or started a burrow.

10) Check fencing daily for breeches until all tortoises have burrows, and then check weekly for 3 months. Barrier fence should remain in place for 6 months or until it decomposes.

Tortoises are usually released within 24 hours of excavation or capture. They are not just "dumped out" in random groups; they should be released in specific locations with the individuals from their original pods. Tortoises are not relocated into areas that have been cleared or just burned with no forage plants available.

How do tortoises adjust when released? They usually run as fast as they can go until they hit a barrier (that is why a fence is needed). Until they get re-oriented to this new habitat they will keep trying to head home. After a while they may check out existing burrows (and get run out by the current resident) or use unoccupied ones. They eventually dig their own burrows (and hope they don't get "abducted by aliens" again).

The recipient site or on-site preserve is usually enclosed in a fence buried 2 feet to keep tortoises from crossing roads or moving into unsuitable areas. If the recipient site is next to a natural area or for some reason a permanent fence is not desired, then the tortoises may be enclosed in a temporary fence of staked hay bales. The tortoises will not burrow out under bales that are completely flush to the ground with no gaps.

Artificial burrows (buried plastic tubes or large diameter pipes) have been used by zoos and parks and for relocations. Forcing multiple tortoises into a burrow is not a good idea and can lead to stress and disease.

How is your habitat managed?

A well-designed tortoise habitat monitoring and management plan includes a prescribed burn plan.

Controlled fire is one of the most important tools we have to manage tortoise habitats which are specifically adapted to having periodic fires. When we can't use fire, then other tools including mechanical clearing or mowing, or very selective use of herbicides, can be used but they do not always produce the best results. We still do not really know the long-term effects that herbicides can have on tortoises.

The frequency of burning for a specific habitat is part of the habitat management plan for a preserve or natural area. Most preserves use a three- to five-year burn schedule. Proper burning will improve the forage and habitat for tortoises, deer, turkey, and quail as well as help deter wildfires. Too frequent burning can actually harm some species, so having and following a plan is important.

Notice the increasing fuel:
- Lots of turkey oak leaves that will turn brown and fall each year
- Lots of pine needles and dead branches
- Lots of volatile rosemary shrubs and palmettos which burn like torches

A fire lane is cut around the areas to be burned. This protects structures (like houses), equipment, and areas the manager does not want to burn. A well-managed fire will not jump the fire lane. Fires must only be started when the weather conditions (wind speed, wind direction, temperature, and humidity) are right.

A well-designed management plan includes management responses to information that will be obtained from monitoring the forage and other habitat parameters of the preserve. For example, if a measurement of tree canopy cover shows continuous increase then planning a burn or thinning trees could be the responses.

Tortoises have been observed eating the charred wood left after a burn. Carbon is well known as a treatment for some poisons, acting to bond with the toxic chemicals.

Will you be here in the future?

Will your children and grandchildren even get to see a living gopher tortoise? That all depends on you.

How can you help tortoises survive?

Education: Educate yourself and others about what gopher tortoises need to survive and to be protected.

Attention: Pay attention to what is happening in your town and your neighborhood. Notice if tortoises are being taken without proper permits or opportunities to be relocated to on-site or off-site preserves.

Action: Notify authorities when the rules are broken and tortoises are in danger. Share information with others and make concern over the gopher tortoise a positive not a negative. Make sure that elected officials know how important it is to protect our natural heritage. Write letters, send e-mails, or call to make sure they know how you feel.

Support: Provide money and volunteer time to help organizations with management of preserves and natural areas so that they are maintained to protect the wildlife.

Here are some things that are important for tortoise survival that you can help with:

- Don't let your cat outside. Cats kill a lot of animals and their owners never know it. They especially are dangerous to baby tortoises.

- Don't let your dog bother tortoises or run where tortoises have burrows. Dogs get excited when they see a crawling tortoise. To them it is like a walking chewbone. Dogs kill thousands of tortoises every year.

- Don't let your friends throw things down into the burrows. They may cause the tortoise to be stuck or be harmed.

- Make sure that people who are clearing land where there are tortoises have a permit from the proper agencies before they destroy any burrows. Without someone checking, many of these people will illegally kill tortoises and destroy their habitat. Call the authorities and let them know what is happening.

- Leave tortoises where you find them, they are not lost. Tortoises know their neighborhoods just as you do and can find their way back. Obviously if they are in danger of being run over or caught up in wire or stuck, it is okay to get them out of trouble, but then put them back in the nearest natural or grassy area.

Gopher tortoises were once very common all over the Southeastern United States, but as more people move to the same habitats that are used by tortoises, they change the habitat and the tortoises cannot survive. Even if the tortoises are left in small areas, they move around so much and need such a large area to forage in that they often wander on to roads and are squashed.

Refer to the books, articles, and papers listed in the bibliography. Many of these are available at local libraries and bookstores. The scientific papers will probably have to be obtained from a university library. If you are really interested in finding additional information, try contacting the following organizations:

Organizations Concerned About Conservation and Research

Gopher Tortoise Conservation Initiative
Ashton Biodiversity Research and Preservation Institute, Inc.
14260 W. Newberry Rd. #331
Newberry, FL 32669
Tortfarm2@aol.com
www.ashtonbiodiversity.org

Society for the Study of Amphibians and Reptiles
http://www.ku.edu/~ssar/organization.html

Gopher Tortoise Council
c/o The Florida Museum of Natural History
P.O. Box 117800
University of Florida
Gainesville, FL 32611
http://www.gophertortoisecouncil.org/

Agencies Responsible for the Protection of Gopher Tortoises

(to get more information and to find out who to call for enforcement and protection)
You can find the local phone numbers and addresses for these agencies in your local or regional directory or by calling information if you do not have access to the Internet.

U.S. Fish and Wildlife Service
Gopher Tortoise Species Coordinator
http://endangered.fws.gov/i/C2V.html

Mississippi Department of Wildlife and
Fish Protection
http://www.mdwfp.com/

Florida Fish and Wildlife Conservation
Commission
http://www.floridaconservation.org/

South Carolina Department of Natural
Resources
http://www.dnr.state.sc.us/

Georgia Department of Natural Resources
http://www.dnr.state.ga.us/

Louisiana Division of Wildlife and
Fisheries
http://www.wlf.state.la.us/

Alabama Department of Natural Resources
http://www.dcnr.state.al.us/agfd/

Animals Named in This Book

Throughout the book we use common names of both plants and animals. The common name we use for a plant or animal may be different than one you may have heard since people give different names to plants and animals depending on what part of the country they live in, their culture, even how their teachers taught them (right or wrong). When we use common names like gopher, it could mean gopher as in the mammal (also called salamander in some areas which can then be confused with the four-legged amphibian of the same name) or it could mean gopher tortoise. To make sure we are all talking about the same organism, we use the "real name" or scientific name. This name is in Latin and was given to the plant or the animal by a scientist who was the first to describe it in the scientific literature. Having the scientific name may help you find out more about the species than just the information that we have included in this book.

The following list of animals is taken from *Gopher Tortoise Relocation Symposium Proceedings* by Dale R. Jackson and Eric G. Milstrey, 1989. (Nongame Wildlife Technical Report #5. Florida Fish and Wildlife Conservation Commission, Tallahassee, Florida). Note that we have added to this list some species that we have found on occasion in gopher tortoise burrows in parts of their range that were not listed by Jackson and Milstrey. Note also that this number system assumes that the species occurs in the area and that the burrow is in the correct habitat (e.g. sandhills) for the species to occur.

1. Very common (1 out of 10 burrows in right habitat)
2. Common (1 out of 20 burrows in right habitat)
3. Uncommon (1out of 30 burrows in right habitat)
4. Rare (1 out of 50 burrows in right habitat)
5. A surprise (1 out of 100 burrows in right habitat)

Amphibians

Common Name	Scientific Name (Genus and species)	Frequency of Occurrence in or near Burrows
Barking Treefrog	*Hyla gratiosa*	4
Florida Gopher Frog	*Rana capito*	1
Greenhouse Frog	*Eleutherodactylus planirostris*	1*
Eastern Narrow-mouthed Toad	*Gastrophryne carolinensis*	4
Eastern Spadefoot	*Scaphiopus holbrooki*	5
Southern Leopard Frog	*Rana sphenocephala*	5
Southern Toad	*Bufo terrestris*	4

*These species are more common in burrows in habitats that have more moisture available such as pine flatwoods.

Animals Named in This Book

Reptiles

Common Name	Scientific Name (Genus and species)	Frequency of Occurrence in or near Burrows
Black Racer	*Coluber constrictor*	2
Crowned Snake	*Tantilla relicta*	4
Eastern Coachwhip	*Masticophis flagellum*	2
Eastern Box Turtle	*Terrapene carolina*	4*
Eastern Coral Snake	*Micrurus fulvius*	2
Eastern Diamondback Rattlesnake	*Crotalus adamanteus*	4
Eastern Garter Snake	*Thamnophis sirtalis*	4
Eastern Hognose	*Heterodon platyrhinos*	4
Eastern Indigo Snake	*Drymarchon corais*	3
Fence Swift	*Sceloporus undulatus*	4
Florida Worm Lizard	*Rhineura floridana*	4
Gopher Tortoise	*Gopherus polyphemus*	
Green Anole	*Anolis carolinensis*	4
Mole Skink	*Eumeces egregius*	2
Pinewoods Snake	*Rhadinaea flavilata*	5*
Pigmy Rattlesnake	*Sistrurus miliarius*	2*
Red Ratsnake	*Elaphe guttata*	3
Southern Hognose	*Heterodon simus*	3

Birds

Common Name	Scientific Name (Genus and species)	Frequency of Occurrence in or near Burrows
Bob White (Quail)	*Colinus virginianus*	2
Burrowing Owl	*Speotyto cunicularia*	5
Ground Dove	*Columbina passerina*	2
Redstart	*Setophaga ruticilla*	5
Palm Warbler	*Dendroica palmarum*	5
Prairie Warbler	*Dendroica discolor*	5

*These species are more common in burrows in habitats that have more moisture available such as pine flatwoods.

Animals Named in This Book

Mammals

Common Name	Scientific Name (Genus and species)	Frequency of Occurrence in or near Burrows
Armadillo	*Dasypus novemcinctus*	1
Cotton Mouse	*Peromyscus gossypinus*	3
Coyote	*Canis latrans*	4
Eastern Cottontail	*Sylvilagus floridanus*	4
Florida Mouse	*Podomys floridanus*	2
Gray Fox	*Urocyon cinereoargenteus*	5
Hispid Cotton Rat	*Sigmodon hispidus*	3*
Old Field Mouse	*Peromyscus polionotus*	1
Opossum	*Didelphis virginiana*	5
Pocket Gopher	*Geomys pinetis*	5
Spotted Skunk	*Spilogale putorius*	3
Striped Skunk	*Mephitis mephitis*	3

Invertebrates

Common Name	Scientific Name (Genus and species)	Frequency of Occurrence in or near Burrows
Ant lions	*(2 species) Myrmeleon sp.*	3
Adhopius Beetle	*Copris gopheri*	3
Black Widow Spider	*Latrodectus mactans*	3
Centipede (3 species)	*Scolopendra spp.*	1
Cob-web House Spider	*Pholcus sp.*	1
Daddy longlegs	*Crosbyella sp.*	2
Funnel Web Spider	*Neoantistea alachua*	1
Gopher (Cave) Crickets	*Ceuthophilus latibuli* and *C.walkeri*	1
Gopher Fly	*Edutrichota gopheri*	3
Gopher Tick	*Amblyomma tuberculatum*	1
Gulf Coast Tick	*Amblyomma maculatum*	5
Gopher Tortoise Aphodius Beetle	*Aphodius troglodytes*	5
Gopher Tortoise Robber Fly	*Machinum polyphemi*	5
Millipedes (4 genera)	*Rinocricis sp.*	1
Tortoise Burrow Dance Fly	*Drapetis sp.*	3
Scorpion	*Centruroides sp.*	3

*These species are more common in burrows in habitats that have more moisture available such as pine flatwoods.

Glossary

Ancient: Very old, maybe thousands of years or more in age.

Apron: The mound of sand shaped like a half circle that spreads outward from the mouth of a tortoise burrow like a front porch.

Aquatic: Living or growing in or on the water.

Arch: A structure shaped like an inverted U or half circle which supports the weight above it and has been used by engineers since ancient times for its strength. The mouth of a tortoise burrow is usually in the shape of an arch.

Assessment: The evaluation of conditions on a site including how many tortoises and other protected species are present as well as the quality of the natural habitat.

Beak: The horny structure covering the tortoise's jaws.

Biodiversity: Bio refers to life or living organisms; diversity refers to their number and variety in a specific location.

Burrow classifications: "Active," "inactive," "very inactive," and "abandoned" are classifications the authors use for designating the state of gopher tortoise burrows. Tortoises, particularly young ones, may be found in any of these burrows; but an abandoned burrow is most likely uninhabited.

Canopy: The uppermost layer in a forest formed by the crown or upper branches of trees, or the area shaded by it. If this area becomes greater than 60% of a site, it may become a problem for gopher tortoises.

Carapace: Top shell or dorsal side of a tortoise or turtle.

Carbon: A chemical element; what remains after carbohydrates or wood burn. It is usually black in color. Carbon has four bonding sites and often is used to bond with toxic chemicals and render them harmless.

Carrion: Dead animals or insects, which are sometimes eaten by tortoises.

Cellulose: The fiber in plants, which is made of a complex carbohydrate called "polysaccharide" (made of many sugars). It provides flexible structure and support in plants. Humans cannot digest cellulose, but many bacteria, round worms, insects, and other specialized herbivores can use it as a source of energy by breaking down its molecules into smaller useable sugars. Tortoises have a microfauna of roundworms and bacteria in their gut that help in the digestion of some of these cellulose molecules. Large portions of plant cellulose still remain undigested and pass out of the tortoise as feces.

Chordate: A taxonomic classification that includes animals that have a hollow dorsal nerve cord and a notochord and pharyngeal gill slits at some stage of development.

Commensal: An organism that lives together with another (as in a tortoise burrow), participating in a symbiotic relationship in which one species derives some benefit while the other is unaffected.

Community: A group of different species of plants and animals which may be interdependent, and which live and interact with one another in a specific area (for example, a sandhill community).

Conservation easement: A legal agreement that a landowner can enter into with a nonprofit conservation agency, county, state, or other regulatory agency that oversees the lands. The agreement can provide cash and tax incentives for the landowner and can provide long-term protection from development. It may also provide for the proper management of natural communities and organisms living on the lands involved including the gopher tortoise. A well-written agreement will allow the landowner to continue most with normal uses of the land within reasonable conservation management guidelines. This is a win-win situation for the landowner and the tortoise.

Environmental consultant: A biologist who is hired by a landowner or developer who wishes to build something on the land that would change the habitat for the wildlife. The consultant conducts surveys, obtains permits, and carries out various activities usually required by federal, state, or local government permits. The consultant is usually well trained in wildlife biology, knows proper field techniques and how to look for wildlife and plants, and understands how to plan appropriately for the needs of the wildlife community as well as for the desired human use of the land.

Controlled burn (also called a prescribed burn): A forest fire that is planned and carefully carried out to use the wind and other factors to make it hot in some locations and cooler in others so it will affect the vegetation to achieve a planned result.

Dermal: refers to skin; it may be a layer of skin or skin tissues, as in the scutes or scales of tortoises and turtles.

Developer: A person or company that oversees and provides the money and plans for building structures on land for human use.

Development: The process of building homes, roads, stores and other things found in human communities.

Donor site: The original site tortoises are removed from (or "donated") in order to be relocated to a recipient site. Land development is often the reason for relocation..

Dorsal: Refers to the top side of something, such as the top shell or carapace of the tortoise.

Ectothermic: An organism whose body temperature is controlled through behavior using the environment to regulate body temperature by moving in and out of the sun or in or out of water. Most reptiles, amphibians, fish, and invertebrates are ectothermic.

End chamber: The final end to the tortoise burrow which is usually enlarged by the tortoise to allow room to move around and rest comfortably. It is well insulated and thus the air in the end chamber usually has a temperature warmer than the air at the mouth of the burrow in winter and cooler than the air at the surface in summer. Because the end chamber is at or near the water table, the air in the end chamber usually has a higher humidity than the air at the mouth of the burrow.

Endangered: A term used to describe the potential for a species to be in danger of becoming extinct. Regulatory agencies apply the term as a specific category to species that have been studied and proposed by experts as being in critical danger of becoming extinct.

Endemic: Something that has been found only in one location (for example, in central Georgia) or in one specific habitat type (for example, in a tortoise burrow).

Endothermic: An organism whose body temperature is controlled internally. Most birds and mammals are endothermic.

Epoxy: A strong glue used to hold a radio transmitter to the shell of a tortoise so the tortoise can be located and studied.

Extinct: Something that has disappeared from the earth forever.

Feces: Solid or semi-solid waste material ("poop"). In tortoises, feces are passed out of the gut through the cloaca.

Fire-maintained habitat: Sandhills, scrub, and savannah grassland habitats are maintained or kept open by the natural occurrence of fire which burns up the fallen leaves, shrubs, tree seedlings, dead, or sick trees and dead plant materials. This opens the floor of the habitat and allows herbaceous plants such as grasses to flourish. Without the fire, the characteristic vegetation of each of these habitats would gradually be replaced by a variety of densely growing trees and shrubs and the habitat would become a forest where tortoises could no longer find the variety of grasses and herbaceous plants they eat.

Fire lane: A wide strip of bare soil opened up to keep fire in the appropriate burn compartment. A fire lane usually prevents a fire from jumping across to another area (unless there is a strong wind or a burning tree falls across the fire lane).

Forage: Used as a verb to describe the act of looking for food; or as a noun to describe the food that the tortoise is looking for or eating.

Genetic diversity: Genes can determine how a particular organism's body will function. Individual organisms receive genes from each parent which pass on certain characteristics. For a population of tortoises to be healthy, they need to have a diversity of genes available within the population; this allows a variety of combinations of characteristics such as immunity from certain diseases, a healthy circulatory system, the ability to withstand hotter summers, a keen sense of smell, etc. In other words, the individuals cannot be too closely related or have a genetic make up that is too similar.

Graze: As a verb, it means to move around and pick out and eat parts of plants (like cows do); as a noun, it refers to the plant material (usually herbaceous parts of plants) being eaten.

GTCI: Gopher Tortoise Conservation Initiative, a program of the Ashton Biodiversity Preservation and Research Institute, Inc., a nonprofit organization dedicated to preserving upland habitats and in doing research that will help preserve them.

Gular: Under the chin; the gular scale of the male tortoise is usually elongated and used in male-to-male interactions to ram and flip the other male tortoise.

Habitat Management Plan: This is a written plan that includes goals for the habitat being managed, ways to monitor or tell if the goals are being met, and then describes how to insure that the habitat will continue to meet those goals. A goal can be to provide good food for gopher tortoises; a way to insure the continuation of that goal can be to burn or cut timber at certain times and in particular ways.

Habitat: A scientific term that describes the land as well as the living and nonliving resources on that land that form a specific community. The place where a tortoise can make its burrow and forage for food and interact with other tortoises is called its habitat.

Harmless: In reference to snakes, it usually refers to snakes that are not poisonous or dangerous to humans.

Glossary

Hatchling: A tortoise that has just left the egg.

Herbivore: An animal that eats mostly plants. Gopher tortoises are herbivores but will occasionally eat carrion and insects.

Herbs: The scientist uses this term to refer to non-woody ferns and flowering plants. Herbaceous plants have tender parts that are eaten by tortoises and other herbivores.

Herpetologist: A biologist that specializes in the study of amphibians and reptiles.

Home range: An area that an animal uses for a period of time and where it finds most of its food, water, and shelter. A tortoise may have one or more burrows in its home range. Occasionally a tortoise or animal will leave its home range and venture out for short trips or may even leave for some period before returning.

Home: A physical place that an animal frequents for shelter; a place that provides protection from weather or from predators.

Invertebrates: Animals without internal skeletons or backbones. Some (such as arthropods) have external skeletons that support their bodies. Mollusks (such as snails), roundworms (such as nematodes), flatworms (such as planarians), segmented worms (such as earthworms or leeches), arthropods (such as arachnids or spiders), millipedes, centipedes, crustaceans (such as crayfish), as well as insects, corals, and sponges are all invertebrates.

Juvenile: Animal that is not sexually mature and cannot mate successfully.

Keystone: A wedge-shaped stone at the top or center of an arch of stones or bricks which holds the arch together. A species of plant or animal that through its actions or presence is key to the health and support of others in its community is termed a keystone species.

Mitigation bank: Funds that are gathered for purchasing tortoise habitats or other conservation lands. Land developers or owners pay this money to a state or federal conservation agency, or sometimes to counties. Funds from a mitigation bank may be used to develop and carry out management plans and monitoring programs to ensure that optimal conditions are sustained for gopher tortoises and other protected species. Mitigation funds are often paid when land is being developed in a way that will harm one or more species and alternatives such as relocating the species or having decent preserves on site are not available.

Nutrients: Chemicals required for survival of an organism, such as carbohydrates, proteins, fats, amino acids, vitamins, and minerals.

Obligates: Organisms that can only live in a certain place (such as a tortoise burrow) because of their particular needs.

Permit application: An application explaining what development is planned on a property and how a protected species will be managed. It is required by the various state agencies where the gopher tortoise is protected by the state. In states where the tortoise is protected by the Fish and Wildlife Service, the application goes to this federal agency.

Pheromones: Chemicals (usually scents) made by an animal's body to attract a mate or mark a territory or stimulate male aggression. Tortoises have a very good sense of smell. Male tortoises produce pheromones in scent glands under their chin.

Plastron: The bottom shell of a turtle or tortoise.

Pod: A term used to describe a group of tortoises found within a specific area. This may be a social group of tortoises that interact with each other on a regular basis. This term is also used by botanists to describe a seed case which holds together a group of seeds ("peas in a pod").

Poisonous: An organism that contains chemicals which may be produced in glands (in the mouth or in a stinger), and which may cause death or illness when eaten or touched.

Population: A group of members of the same species that are living in a defined area.

Prescribed burn: A burn plan that is developed after reviewing monitoring data to help meet the management goals for a site. For example, if the canopy and shrub layers cover more that 60% of the ground, then the burn would be set and managed to reduce both the shrub and tree layers.

Radio transmitter: A device that runs on batteries and sends out a signal on a radio frequency that can be detected by a receiver.

Recipient site: A habitat or location tortoises are moved to from their original or donor site.

Refuge: A place of safety; a place where an animal can survive during a drought, or flood, or freezing weather or fire.

Relocation permit: A term used by regulatory agencies to describe a permit that allows the holder to capture or excavate and remove a certain number of tortoises, take their habitat, and destroy their burrows. The tortoises to be relocated must be removed from the donor site and placed on an appropriately managed recipient site using certain guidelines.

Remnant: A leftover piece or part of something; as in a remnant piece of property or the remnants of an animal population.

Reptile: A taxonomic classification of vertebrate animals in the Phylum Chordata and in the Class Reptilia that have scales, are ectothermic, and usually lay eggs. Reptiles include the very primitive tuatara, the turtles and tortoises, the crocodiles and alligators, and the snakes and lizards.

Savannah: A grassland with scattered trees.

Scute: The horny, skin plates or scales over the tortoise's bony shell.

Slither: To slide or crawl, as in the movement of a snake or lizard or worm.

Slope: The slant or inclination of an object such as a hillside, board, or ramp. A 3:1 slope is one that drops 1 foot for every 3 feet of length.

Spring scale: A scale with a spring inside that stretches when there is a weight on the hook end. It will stretch a certain length depending on the weight. This is marked by a pointer that points to the number of grams or kilograms the tortoise weighs.

Sustainability: The ability of a place or habitat to retain its characteristics over time.

Take permit: Permit that allows its holder to clear a piece of land. Often, "takes" involve the destruction of tortoise burrows and habitats and the killing of the tortoises on a site, often by bulldozing. To obtain this permit, landowners must provide a report demonstrating how development will avoid negative impacts to the protected species and how he will mitigate these potential impacts. In the state of Florida, these permits actually allow landowners to eliminate the population of protected species on a site after mitigation fees have been submitted.

Take: Term used by regulatory agencies to describe the illegal action of killing a protected species, its nest, or burrow, or to otherwise hinder the species in violation of the Endangered Species Act.

Terrestrial: Living or growing in, on, or near land..

Testudines: A taxonomic classification; the order of Reptiles that includes turtles and tortoises and is characterized by fused ribs and backbone that forms a bony carapace and plastron (shell) which is covered by dermal scales.

Testudinidae: A taxonomic classification; the family of the order Testudines that includes land tortoises like the gopher tortoise.

Transects: Imaginary divisions of a land area. Lines are drawn on a map along compass headings in order to gather data such as how many tortoises there are or how much forage is available in a given location..

Uplands: A specific term used to describe the habitats found on higher, well-drained sandy soils. Many upland habitats have characteristic vegetation that makes them well-suited for the gopher tortoise. These well-drained soils have been a target of development; the natural upland habitats are being rapidly destroyed and redesigned for human use. Developers generally remove all vegetation from the upland property and bring in non-native landscape plants that forever alter the natural associations between plants, insects, tortoises, birds, and other animals that live there.

URTD: Upper Respiratory Tract Disease. In tortoises, it is caused by a bacterium called *Mycoplasma agassizii* and several other strains. It may kill or make tortoises very sick. There is no known cure.

Ventral: The underside of something, such as the plastron or belly side of a tortoise.

Xeric: A very dry habitat.

Bibliography

* Indicates general references we recommend for those interested in turtles.

Ashton, R.E. and Ashton, P.S. "*Gopherus polyphemus* (Gopher Tortoise) Use of Abandoned Burrows," *Herpetological Review,* vol. 32 (2001): pp. 185–6.

*———. *Handbook of Reptiles and Amphibians of Florida, Part 2: Lizards, Turtles, and Crocodilians.* Miami, Florida: Windward Press, 1991 (rev.).

Ashton, R.E.and Ashton, K.J. "Drinking Behavior in Gopher Tortoises," *Herpetological Review*, vol. 22 (1992): pp.55–6.

Ashton, R. E., Ashton, P.S., and Mosura-Bliss, E. L. "Tortoise Management as Urbanization Encroaches," *Proceedings of North American Tortoise Conference, Publicaciones de la Sociedad Herpetológica Mexicana,* vol. 2 (1994): pp. 210–13.

Auffenberg, W. *Tortoise Behavior and Survival.* Chicago, Ilinois: Rand McNally, 1969.

———. "Florida Environments and their Herpetofaunas, Part II: Changes in their Environment," *Florida Herpetologist,* no. 3.

Berish, Joan E. *Management Considerations for the Gopher Tortoise in Florida.* Tallahassee, Florida: Florida Fish and Wildlife Conservation Commission, 2001.

Cox, J., Inkley, D., and Kautz, R. "Ecology and habitat protection needs of gopher tortoise *(Gopherus polyphemus)* populations found on lands slated for large-scale development in Florida," *Florida Game and Fresh Water Fish Commission Nongame Wildlife Program Technical Report,* no. 4. (1997).

Deimer, J.E. "The Ecology and Management of the Gopher Tortoise in the Southeastern United States," *Herpetologica,* vol. 42 (1986): pp. 125–33.

———. "Home Range and Movements of the Tortoise *Gopherus polyphemus* in northern Florida," *Journal of Herpetology*, vol. 26 (1992): pp. 158–65.

Dodd, C. K. Jr., Ashton, R. E. Jr., Franz, R., and Wester, E. (editors). "Burrow associates of the gopher tortoise," *Proceedings of the 8th Annual Meeting of the Gopher Tortoise Council,* (1990): pp. 134.

*Ernst, C. H. and Barbour, R. W. *Turtles of the World.* Washington, District of Columbia: Smithsonian Institution, 1989.

*Ernst, C. H., Barbour, R. W., and Lovich, J.E. *Turtles of the United States and Canada.* Washington, District of Columbia: Smithsonian Institution, 1994.

Hansen, K. "The burrow of the gopher tortoise," *Journal of the Florida Academy of Science,* vol. 26 (1963): pp. 353–60.

Harless, M. and Morlock, H. (editors). *Turtles, Perspectives and Research.* Malabar, Florida: Krieger Publishing, 1989.

Hayes, M.P. and LeCorff, J. *"Gopherus polyphemus* (gopher tortoise) food," *Herpetological Review,* vol. 20 (1989).

Iverson, J. B. "The reproductive biology of *Gopherus polyphemus* (Chelonia: Testudinidae)," *American Midland Naturalist,* vol. 103 (1980): pp. 353–59.

Jackson, D. R. and Milstrey, E. G. "The fauna of gopher tortoise burrows," *Gopher Tortoise Relocation Symposium Proceedings Technical Report No. 5.* (1989): pp: 86–98.

Jones, C. and Franz, R.. "Use of Gopher Tortoise Burrows by Florida Mice *(Podomys floridanus)* in Putnam County," *Florida Scientist,* vol. 18 (1990): pp. 45–51.

Macdonald, L.A. and Mushinsky, H.R. "Foraging Ecology of the Gopher Tortoise in a Sandhill Habitat," *Herpetologica,* vol. 44 (1988): pp. 345–53.

McCoy, E. D. and Mushinsky, H. R. "Studying a Species In Decline: Gopher Tortoises and the Dilemma of 'Correction Factors,' " *Herpetologica,* vol. 48 (1992): pp. 402–7.

McRae, W.A., Landers, J.L., and Garner, J.A. "Movement patterns and home range of the gopher tortoise," *American Midland Naturalist,* vol. 106 (1981): pp. 521–5.

Means, D. B. "Responses to Winter Burrow Flooding of the Gopher Tortoise *(Gopherus polyphemus Daudin),*" *Herpetologica*, vol. 38 (1982): pp. 521–5.

Milstrey, E. G. "Ticks and invertebrate commensals in gopher tortoise burrows: implications and importance," *Proceedings of the Annual Meeting of the Gopher Tortoise Council* (1988): pp. 4–15.

Mushinsky, H. R. and Esman, L.A. "Perceptions of gopher tortoise burrows over time," *Florida Field Naturalist*, vol. 22 (1994): pp. 1–7.

Wilson, D. S., Mushinsky, H.R., and McCoy, E.D. "Home range, activity, and burrow use of juvenile gopher tortoises *(Gopherus polyphemus)* in a central Florida population." In *Biology of North American Tortoises* by R. B. Bury and D.J. Germano, eds. Washington, District of Columbia: U.S. Department of Interior National Biological Survey, Fish and Wildlife Research 13, pp. 147-60.

Wilson, D. S., Mushinsky, H. R., and McCoy, E. D. "Relationship between gopher tortoise body size and burrow width," *Herpetological Review*, vol. 22 (1991): pp. 122–4.

Credits for Photography and Drawings

Taking photographs of tortoises and their activities is very time-consuming and requires a lot of patience and luck. Some of the photographs in this book are exactly as any photographer today would have wanted, while others date back nearly 30 years and were taken under less than ideal conditions. Shots of tortoise activities are sometimes the best we could get after many, many hours of following tortoises and trying to catch them doing the activities we wanted to illustrate. Both authors have been wildlife photographers for many years and are aware of the tricks and methods for getting certain animal photographs. Keep in mind that these are all wild gopher tortoise photographs and not photographs of captive tortoises. The authors worked with GTCI interns and in particular with intern Milena Scholtens Moreira from the Netherlands on obtaining some of the shots. Milena spent many hours working with the authors on catching these wild tortoises in the right pose or finding the correct light and position for a particular shot.

Unless otherwise noted, all photographs are the property of or were taken by Patricia Sawyer Ashton or Ray E. Ashton Jr. Special note is made of the wonderful artistic contribution by well-known scientific illustrator and wildlife photographer David Dennis. David drew the gopher tortoise at the mouth of its burrow for GTCI's Gopher Tortoise Reserve Sign. He also provided the following images: page 5 (skeleton drawing), page 21 (Black racer), and pages 22 and 24 (Gopher cricket).

Also, Christen Noble, an intern from the state of Washington, has assisted with taking and preparing photographs and with proofreading.

If you enjoyed reading this book, here are some other books from Pineapple Press on related topics. Ask your local bookseller for our books. For a complete catalog, write to Pineapple Press, P.O. Box 3889, Sarasota, FL 34230 or call 1-800-PINEAPL (746-3275). Or visit our website at www.pineapplepress.com.

The Crafts of Florida's First People by Robin Brown. Learn how to throw spears and darts, make pottery, weave cloth, mix paint, build traps, and even how to start a fire without matches—just the way Florida's first people did it for thousands of years. Full color; for readers ages 10 and up. ISBN 1-56164-282-7 (pb)

The Exploring Wild series: A series of field guides, each with information on all the parks, preserves, and natural areas in its region, including wildlife to look for and best time of year to visit. Includes *Exploring Wild North Florida* (ISBN 1-56164-091-3, pb) and *Exploring Wild Northwest Florida* by Gil Nelson (ISBN 1-56164-086-7, pb); *Exploring Wild South Florida* by Susan D. Jewell. (ISBN 1-56164-125-1, pb).

Florida A to Z by Susan Jane Ryan. Crammed into colorful illustration and photo collages—one for each letter of the alphabet—are almost two hundred facts about Florida personalities, history, geography, nature, and culture. Full color; for readers ages 8–12. ISBN 1-56164-249-5 (hb)

The Florida Water Story by Peggy Sias Lantz and Wendy A. Hale. Illustrates and describes many of the plants and animals that depend on the springs, rivers, beaches, marshes, and reefs in and around Florida, including corals, sharks, lobsters, alligators, manatees, birds, and turtles. 2-color illustrations throughout; for readers ages 10–14. ISBN 1-56164-099-9 (hb)

Sinkholes by Sandra Friend. What is a sinkhole? Far from being just a hole in the ground, a sinkhole is a very special type of natural phenomenon. Aimed at readers ages 12 and up, this book describes how sinkholes occur, the types of sinkholes, and the variety of plants and animals they support. Full color; readers ages 12 and up. ISBN 1-56164-258-4 (hb)

The Southern Fossil Discoveries series by Judy Cutchins and Ginny Johnston. Explores the prehistoric animals that once lived in the coastal lowlands and Southern forests and seas, describing how they looked, how they lived, and what they ate. Includes *Ice Age Giants of the South* (ISBN 1-56164-195-2, hb), *Giant Predators of the Ancient Seas* (ISBN 1-56164-237-1, hb), and *Dinosaurs of the South* (ISBN 1-56164-266-5, hb). Full-color photos of fossil bones, reconstructed skeletons, and lifelike models of extinct creatures. Full color; readers ages 8–12.

The Young Naturalist's Guide to Florida by Peggy Sias Lantz and Wendy A. Hale. Plants, birds, insects, reptiles, and mammals are all around us. This enticing book shows you where and how to look for Florida's most interesting natural features and creatures. Step-by-step drawings for 60 subjects; suitable for all ages. ISBN 1-56164-051-4 (pb)